Life Before Life

Life Before Life

by Sarah Hinze

ISBN: 1-55517-092-7
Library of Congress Catalog Card Number: 93-72499

Requests for such permissions should be addressed to:

CFI
Cedar Fort, Incorporated
925 North Main, Springville, UT 84663 801-489-4084

1 2 3 4 5 6 7 8 9 10

Cover Design by Lyle Mortimer
Typeset by Brian Carter
Manufactured in the United States of America

This book is printed on acid-free paper.

In Memory of

Joyce Alger Straley, whose constant prayers were for this book and who died June 29, 1991. Her loving presence has been felt in the progress of this work and especially in its completion.

Dedication

It is to the pre-born, the multitudes of pure
and holy spirits waiting to come to this earth, that
I dedicate this work.

To anyone who has ever uttered the words, "Haven't we met somewhere before?", *Life Before Life*'s message will strike a familiar chord.

I can attest to the truthfulness of this book, not only through my personal experience with my own pre-born child, but also through my work with the many women of Arizona Eagle Forum. These women work so diligently for God, home and country, and their familiar faces, no matter where my travels may take me, always seem to welcome me home.

—Joan Payne
President, Arizona Eagle Forum

Life Before Life reinforces our belief of existence before earth life with powerful, yet tender, accounts from the lives of spiritually aware people.

In a world where life has little meaning and regard, Sarah Hinze has brought us a collection of true life stories that reinforce the fact that life is God-given, is of the utmost importance and does exist before birth.

—Elaine Hatch
wife of Senator Orrin G. Hatch

Life Before Life is a fascinating collection of stories, songs and poems. At a time when the very moral fabric of our nation is being ripped to shreds, it is heartwarming to know that there are individuals who still feel and care very much about keeping our moral standards high. One of these individuals in Sarah Hinze. Very few authors today have caught the vision of what America used to be and was meant to be. Sarah Hinze has that vision and it is openly displayed upon the pages of this collection.

Life Before Life captures the vision of the ideal heart in America. This book underscores the deep spiritual and temporal commitment to the unborn. One cannot avoid the deep spiritual feeling expressed page after page in this work. Many of the stories that Sarah Hinze has collected in this beneficial book touch the heart as well as the mind.

Life Before Life is another weapon in the arsenal of the righteous. Those who feel a deep-rooted conviction to protect and preserve the unborn will cherish this work. One cannot walk away from this book without having their pro-life stance strengthened and their pro-choice stance weakened. For those who may say this is just more pro-life propaganda, think again. Read the story, "My Angel Wrapped in Light." It will touch the heart where other forms of communication have been less successful.

As an adopted child of the 1950's era, I can truly appreciate the need to teach our people the alternative to abortion. My birth mother chose life for me and what a sacrifice she made. I was certainly not convenient, nor planned, but true to her conviction, she gave me a chance at life. My parents are grateful to this woman who gave me that opportunity, for a fine family we have made because adoption was chosen instead of abortion.

Sarah Hinze has been guided by the Lord to offer each of us an opportunity to recommit ourselves to the struggle to stop the slaughter of our unborn children. Surely, the Lord will bless us as we assume our responsibilities to stop this destruction of innocent human life. We can no longer sit on the sidelines, we must enter the race to rescue the helpless. *Life Before Life* will help put the fire in your heart, the spiritual strength in your mind and the desire to arm yourself in this most holy of wars, Pro-Life versus Pro-Choice.

—Mark W. Killian
State Representative
District 30,
Arizona House Majority Leader

In her quest to find the correlation between God and Man, Sarah Hinze forces us to look behind the veil. Ecclesiastes 12:7 teaches us that the dust from which we are made shall return to the earth from whence it came, and "the spirit shall return to God Who gave it." In John 17:5, when Jesus was reporting to our Heavenly Father, He said, "And now, Father, glorify Me along with Yourself and restore Me to such majesty and honor in Your presence as I had with you before the world existed." (Amplified Bible). Without question God's Word teaches life before birth with the same surety that it teaches life after death." In our fascination for the hereafter little has been done in researching the time before the spirit comes into the body. Sarah Hinze is to be commended and congratulated for this challenging study.

—Donald N. Sills, D.D.
Chaplain, World Conference of Mayors
Washington, D.C.

Table of Contents

The most important person on earth is a mother. She cannot claim the honor of having built Notre Dame Cathedral. She need not. She has built something more magnificent than any cathedral—a dwelling for an immortal soul, the tiny perfection of her baby's body...The angels have not been blessed with such a grace. They cannot share in God's creative miracle to bring new saints to Heaven. Only a human mother can. Mothers are closer to God the Creator than any other creature; God joins forces with mothers in performing this act of creation...What on God's good earth is more glorious than this: to be a mother?

—Joseph Cardinal Mindszenty

Introduction

You may have noticed that the title of this book is a variation of Dr. Raymond Moody's book, *Life After Life*: a synopsis of various people's "near death" experiences, in which they tell of what they encountered between the time they became clinically dead and then revived. Other books have been written on this subject as well. George Ritchie's *Return from Tomorrow* and Lee Nelson's *Beyond the Veil* series are excellent examples. These first-hand accounts confirm what nearly every religion teaches regarding a continuation of life after death, minus a physical tabernacle (not to say that the separated body and spirit will not be reunited at resurrection day). These testimonials have underscored the importance of unconditional love and service in this life and have de-emphasized the pursuit of worldly wealth and fame. These unique witnesses have impacted mankind in a profound way by empowering the Christian walk with their infectious zeal for love, beauty and goodness.

Life Before Life is similar to these others, in that it deals with the spirit half of our current spirit-body make-up. Only this book deals with the pre-birth side of this life, rather than the post-death side. And these testimonials are not brought to us directly by the yet-to-be-born, but indirectly by those with whom these pre-birth angels have communicated. The accounts in *Life Before Life* are from parents or families who have had some form of profound communication with their pre-born children or siblings. In these pages are a collection of nearly forty stories of people who have seen, heard, or felt the presence of their children before they were born—or even conceived. Some of these experiences have come as visions, dreams or whisperings about a child yet to come to earth. Others have come in flashbacks, prayer experiences, or precious memories of a previous heavenly life.

These accounts make a powerful statement about the sanctity of life and its origins. The earthly tabernacles conceived in the procreative process may be a mere "sublime growth of tissue" in the womb of a mother, but the independent spirit that enters that body by the time of birth is a unique person with individuality like anyone else. The spirit that enters the body by the time of birth is just as real as the spirit that leaves the body upon the death of the mortal tabernacle.

Because these stories are such a spiritual experience for those involved, they are not commonly shared openly, and therefore this phenomenon is not widely known—similar to what had been the case with the "near death" experiences. But just as the publication of the life after life accounts has enriched those who would not have been able to benefit from these beautiful experiences, so also is my hope that the publication of these life before life experiences will begin to have the same effect of enriching mankind's understanding of his godly heritage and the sanctity of all life.

—Sarah Hinze

A Miracle Named Brytnee

At one time or another we are all faced with a decision that will drastically change our lives forever. Sometimes we aren't sure if these changes will be for better or for worse. My time came about two and a half years ago.

My husband, Mark, and I bought a small two-story town-home after we had been married about six months. I was so thrilled as I began transforming this house into our home. We only planned to live in this house for five years or so. Then we hoped to sell our home and buy a new one to begin our family. The Lord apparently had different plans.

One day I realized there was a possibility that I might be pregnant. I did not get too disturbed since I was not positive. I waited about two more weeks and then I was worried. This was terrible in my eyes. I could not possibly have a baby now because I simply was not ready—not financially and certainly not emotionally. That night I knelt down to say my prayers, but still my heart was heavy. As I said my usual prayers, blessing my family and friends, I decided to share my feelings with my Heavenly Father. As I prayed, I explained to the Lord what a mistake I thought a baby would be right now and that I did not want to have one yet. As soon as the words escaped my lips, a feeling of guilt overcame my entire body. I quickly ended my prayer and jumped into bed. Before I fell asleep that night, I knew I had crossed the line.

They will ask you where you are going. Your answer: The place from which I came. I return to that place.

—*First Apocalypse of James 34:17-19*

That same night, I had a dream that would change my whole perspective on life. I dreamed I was in heaven dressed in all white. I was talking with a distant voice, when I saw a beautiful, young girl. She wore a white dress with an enormous white bow in her long, dark hair, and she had the most beautiful brown eyes. I spoke to the voice and said, "Who is that little girl?"

The voice replied, "She is a spirit child waiting for her turn on earth."

I then asked, "Well, if she is going to earth, she should be happy? Why does this little girl look so sad?"

The distant voice answered, "She is upset because

she sees how sad you are that she is coming."

I woke up the next morning knowing that I had hurt my unborn child. From that day forward, I begged the Lord for forgiveness and told him to tell my daughter I wanted her, and I was waiting for her. Several days later, I found out I was not pregnant. Days went by, and I became depressed. I felt I had let my baby down as well as my Heavenly Father. I prayed day and night that the Lord would send me a baby. I was truly sorry for what I had said.

Several weeks passed, and I was sitting in my college history course, when I realized my right leg was numb. I became concerned, so I went to a pay phone to call my doctor. The nurse suggested I come in immediately. I followed her advice and went in. I will never forget how as I drove to the emergency center that night, I felt like something was really wrong. The doctor only told me what I already knew. I was loosing the feeling in my leg and my back. He referred me back to my primary physician, who then referred me to a specialist in neurology.

I waited a week to see a neurologist, and by that time, I was very sick. When I finally got in to see the neurologist, he gave me an examination. He ran some

MY LITTLE CHILD

In your eyes, I see heaven's sun-
  light glowing;
You were there just yesterday.
And I know, that deep inside
  you're knowing,
Why you left that home and came
  to Earth to stay.
There are dreams to last a life-
  time;
There are wonders yet to see,
I see mountains yet unconquered;
I see all that you can be.

Chorus:
You're an angel from above,
Sent to me by One who loves us.
To learn and grow and come to be
A sacred trust He's given me.
To watch and care for you,
And to guide and show the way to,
To form a bond that's meant to
  be,
Forever through eternity,
My little child.

You've been born in a world
  where pain and sorrow,
Seem at times too much to bear.
But you know, that the skies will

clear tomorrow;
You can walk with hope and love
*   enough to share.*
You'll go on, ever nearer,
Every step along the way,
Over coming and fulfilling,
Till you reach the perfect day.

—Afterglow
(Kevin Peay and Joel
McCausland)

tests and assured me that everything would be okay. I was not so sure. I drove home that day, and I wondered what could possibly be wrong with me. Somehow I was comforted.

The following day, I got a phone call from my neurologist. He explained that after seeing the results from my tests, he was led to believe that I had a disease called Multiple Sclerosis (MS). I was shocked to find out that MS is a disease that attacks the Central Nervous System. But nothing could prepare me for what he said next.

He told me I was pregnant.

My life seemed to be crumbling all around me. However, I still found comfort. And the doctor was satisfied that I was not in any real danger at the time.

Several weeks passed, but I continued to get worse. Before long, I could barely walk—even with the aid of a cane. My doctor became concerned that there was a chance I might have a tumor in my spinal cord, in which case I would need surgery immediately. My doctor feared that if I had a tumor, there was a possibility that I would not make it through the pregnancy.

I was faced with the most difficult choice of my life. And unfortunately, with my other medical difficulties, my doctors agreed I needed to do what was best for *me*. They also agreed that I should terminate the pregnancy so they could determine what my problem was. It might also be in my best interest to try getting pregnant again later: after they knew I was okay. I was devastated. How could anyone ask me to choose between my life and my baby's?

I immediately turned to my family for guidance. I found that a portion of my family found themselves blinded by their love for me and felt I should follow the counsel of my physicians. Other family members gave me my space and encouraged me to decide for myself.

I chose to have the baby.

In the end, my whole family supported my choice, and they helped me in my time of need. One thing was certain: my family loved me very much, and I was thankful for that.

I sought the counsel of my church leader for a religious perspective concerning abortion. He encouraged me to pray and have faith that I should make the choice my Heavenly Father wanted. I asked my husband, my father, and my brother to give me a blessing. As they laid their hands on my head and administered to me, I was at peace; and for the first time, I wasn't afraid. I was ready to give up my life for this child, and no one could con-

Our birth is but a sleep and a forgetting:
The Soul that rises with us, our life's Star,
Hath had elsewhere its setting,
And cometh from afar:
Not in entire forgetfulness,
And not in utter nakedness,
But trailing clouds of glory do we come
From God, who is our home:
Heaven lies about us in our infancy!

—William Wordsworth
"Ode on Intimations of Immortality."

vince me otherwise.

I finally consented to have the necessary tests to check for a tumor. After much prayer and fasting, Mark and I knew it would be useless for both the baby and I to die. Each time I was tested, I had to sign away the life of this precious child, but I prayed with all my heart that she would be protected. And she was. The tests showed that I did not have a tumor. The initial diagnosis was upheld: I had MS.

Throughout the rest of my pregnancy, I was hopeful that the baby would be healthy. At times, I felt fear and doubt, but through prayer I was able to overcome those feelings. I knew I had made the right choice. I knew this baby was meant to be.

My condition grew progressively worse, and I feared I would be permanently confined to a wheelchair. I prayed to Heavenly Father that he would allow me to raise my daughter without the use of my chair. So far he has.

My daughter was born a very healthy 6 pounds, 12 ounces. In spite of all our fears, Brytnee has no medical problems.

It has been about two years since all this happened. But it feels like only yesterday. I thank my Heavenly

I came from the house of my father, from a far land. I shall mount up until I return to the land of the pure.

—Psalms of Thomas 17:3-10

Father each day for his guidance and blessings during my pregnancy. The Lord knew I would have to be strong to withstand the hardships that lay ahead. He held my daughter in the hollow of his hand, and has always, always comforted me.

—Jana B.

O my Father, thou that dwellest
In the high and glorious place!
When shall I regain thy presence,
And again behold thy face?
In thy holy habitation
Did my spirit once reside;
In my first primeval childhood
Was I nurtured near thy side.

For a wise and glorious purpose
Thou has placed me here on earth,
And withheld the recollection
Of my former friends and birth,
Yet, ofttimes a secret something
Whispered, "You're a stranger here,"
And I felt that I had wandered
From a more exalted sphere.

—Eliza R. Snow

Kidnapped, Abandoned, but not Alone

October 7, 1986 started out as an ordinary Tuesday in the Skidmore home. Stacy and Robert went to school; Dad went to work. He and Rhonda, his wife, had no idea how trying the following days would be.

Mark's phone rang at 1:45 pm. It was Rhonda: obviously very upset. "I don't know how to tell you...." Her voice trailed off. "Something terrible has happened." There was a pause, and some crying. Then: "Oh Mark, they've taken our Sarah!"

Rhonda had been watching her pre-school children and a neighbor boy. Suddenly the phone rang and her son, Robert, needed her to go to the school. Gathering all the children in the car, she headed out. When she arrived, she ran in and took care of Robert and came back out. When Rhonda returned to the car, the five-year-old boy innocently looked at her and said, "A man took Sarah out of the car."

"That's not funny. Stop playing around," Rhonda scolded.

Again, with a serious face and big eyes he said, "A man took Sarah out of the car."

This time she knew he was not teasing. She could not see her precious three-year-old anywhere! Rhonda's heart sank like an anvil in quicksand.

Returning to the school office, trying frantically not to panic, Rhonda reported the incident. Soon the nurse, the principal and other office ladies were right there to help. "I left Sarah and the other kids in the car unprotected," Rhonda lamented to herself. Her mind blurred, she could not remember Mark's work number, so the office ladies found his number and called him. Rushing to the school, Mark found the police already there, trying to get the story straight from a bewildered Rhonda, who wished in desperation to believe that this was not really happening.

The principal took the children home, and a church leader's family fed and took care of them, while the rattled parents went to the police station. Mark and Rhonda answered questions for the police and the F.B.I.

late into the evening. "Do you know anyone who might want to take Sarah?" Mark and Rhonda could think of no one. All the while, they silently prayed that the Lord would help and protect Sarah wherever she was, and give them the strength to endure. It was useless to think of the possibilities of what might be happening to Sarah. They had to trust Sarah to God's hands while they did what little they could. They cried with fear, not knowing if they would ever see her again in this life. Was she hurt? afraid? Not knowing was the hardest part.

As the children were eating dinner, they asked what Sarah was eating and wondered if the bad man was even feeding her. Little Bobby went outside and called, "Sarah! Sarah!" until his innocent, quivering voice was entirely spent.

The police said that intense media coverage can scare a kidnaper into letting the victim go. The first press conference lasted about 20 minutes. An outraged and saddened Arizona, metropolitan community united their sympathetic hearts and trained their eyes on their televisions as reporters asked the Skidmores about what happened. The Skidmores' plea: "Help us find Sarah." To the kidnaper it was: "Let our little girl go. Drop her off at a street corner or supermarket or anywhere, and she

All souls are prepared before the foundation of the world.

—The Book of Enoch The Apocrypha and Pseude- pigrapha of the Old Testament

Long time before
I in my Mother's Womb was born,
A GOD preparing did this
  Glorious Store,
The World for me adorne.
Into this Eden so Divine and fair
So Wide and Bright, I come his
  Son and Heir.

("The Salutation," The Poetical
Works of Thomas Traherne, ed.
Gladys I. Wade, London, P. J. &
A. E. Dobell, 1932, p. 4.)

will be just fine. We just want our little girl back."

Arriving home late that night, a bedraggled couple found all their children asleep. Turning to the Lord in prayer, the broken couple sought help and comfort. In acting as voice at this critical time, Mark was scared that his highly emotional condition and his intense desire for Sarah's safe return might bias his ability to discern true promptings from the Spirit of God. At first, the prayer centered around consoling Rhonda: that she was not at fault. Mark was also given a glimpse of the anguish of the kidnapper, who surely felt extreme guilt for his act. Mark next wanted to assure Rhonda that Sarah would be okay, but he couldn't. He was constrained. This frightened him. Just one month prior, he had tried to assure Rhonda in a prayer concerning her pregnancy: that the baby would be born healthy and well. Then too, he had been restrained from saying this. Rhonda had a miscarriage five days later. Was Sarah not going to be coming home? Why couldn't he form the words?

At the time of the kidnapping, while their mother had run into the school to tend to Robert's needs, Sarah, two-year-old Heather, and the neighbor boy were playing on the seats and hiding on the floor of the car. Sarah was sitting on the driver's seat with the window rolled down.

A rough-looking man approached the car. He had long, curly, dark hair with a mustache and beard.

"You're coming with me," he said.

Sarah said "No."

The man then reached into the car and pulled her out through the window. She did not scream or kick as he carried her to his dark-brown truck. He put her in the truck and told her to lay on the floor. It was hard and uncomfortable. He drove for a while without saying a word or listening to the radio. They went on a curvy, bumpy road and stopped. After treating her badly, he opened the door and she jumped out. She walked away from the truck, and he made no attempt to stop her. He drove away, and she never saw him again. This entire experience with the "bad man" lasted probably less than an hour.

Sarah walked away from the dirt road and went to a bunch of trees and sat down. She did not cry or try to follow the road back to the highway. She just stayed "in the trees." "I just knowed what to do," she later reported. Barefoot and pantless, she was scratched by the cacti and her little feet were sore and punctured as she determinedly walked the long distance to the trees. She knew where to go even though she could not see the trees from the

She promised me when she was
  here
She'd be my mother—it was
  clear—
But she forgot.

In dreams I tried to help her see
How much her child I longed to
  be—
And then she knew.

Earth life is such a happy place
As I look up at Mother's face—
I love you, Mom!

—*Barbara G. Dykstra*
Copyright © 1993
(Used by Permission)

road. She knew she had to stay by those trees and should not move.

When it got dark, she went to sleep. Awaking when it was yet dark, Sarah was alone and scared. She then saw a small child in the desert. She had short, blond hair and slightly resembled her little sister, Heather. The little girl was wearing a white robe that looked like a T-shirt. She was surrounded or encircled by a brilliant light. Sarah thought the leaves of the trees would catch fire because it was so bright. When later asked how she could see this personage, Sarah said "In my eyes. She wasn't really in the desert but she wasn't in my mind either. I didn't pretend. I could see her in my eyes." The shining girl of comfort just stood there and did not speak to her. Sarah stayed by the trees and did not move for 2 days but was constantly attended.

Mark continued his prayer, grasping for words of comfort by speaking of a loving Heavenly Father, who is fully aware of all events. Then his voice seemed to change. It was more of a pure tone and much calmer than his normal voice. His throat felt different too; almost smooth. The words started to flow almost spontaneously so that it seemed that he too was listening to them. Mark remarked how special Sarah was and that

A Sweet, new blossom of
Humanity,
Fresh fallen from God's own
home to flower on earth.

—Geral Massey from "Wooed
and Won"

there was much yet for her to do in this life.

Then Mark began weeping as he anticipated what he was being wrought to say next. This lasted for some time. Finally the composure and the welcome words came: "Sarah is alive and well. She is protected from evil and the deeds of evil men. There are angels attending her and protecting her from harm. There is no power on Earth or Heaven that can or will harm her. Sarah is good and good will always win over evil. Sarah will return to you and grow up in your household and be your little girl again." This was followed by tears of joy and rejoicing. Mark understood why he could not say that Sarah would be okay at first. "The first time, I wanted to say the words but couldn't. The second time, the Lord wanted to say them and did."

For them, the trial was already over—just ten long and lonely hours after she was taken. This grateful and serene couple then astounded a concerned community by their calmness, as the ordeal dragged on for three more days. They talked to numerous news people and were able to tell them that they had full confidence that Sarah would return safely.

Having a premonition that Sarah would return on Friday, the Skidmores spent Wednesday and Thursday

Every baby born into the world is a finer one than the last.

—Charles Dickens
Nicholas Nickleby

*...We say "All this hath been
    before,
All this hath been, I know not
    when or where."
So, friend, when first I looked
    upon your face,
Our thought gave answer, each to
    each, so true,
Opposed mirrors each reflecting
    each—
Altho' I knew not in what time or
    place,
Methought that I had often met
    with you,
And lived in each other's mind
    and speech.*

—Alfred, Lord Tennyson
    "Early Sonnet"
    Poems of Tennyson

just waiting. They tried to get back to a partial routine. By this time, the whole community was involved and posters were going up all over the state. Over $21,000 in reward money was pledged and is still being offered for the arrest of the abductor. People they did not even know donated thousands of dollars to the reward and offered time and services printing and distributing posters and searching.

Thursday night it rained hard; and it was cold. The Skidmores prayed that Sarah would be kept dry and warm. Mark told Rhonda "If the Lord could part the Red Sea, He certainly can part a few raindrops."

Sarah was a little hungry and thirsty but did not eat or drink anything. Thursday night, during the downpour, Sarah said the trees protected her, and she did not get wet. She could put her feet out in the rain and pull them back in out of the rain.

Friday morning, Sarah left her place of refuge and began walking. She did not try to retrace her steps but took a new route. She recounts, "I knowed I had to walk." She said Heavenly Father helped her know which way to go. She walked from early morning until 9:00 am when she heard a loud noise. It was the gun of a quail hunter. Friday was the opening day of quail season. She stood by and waited to see what the hunter (Zane Bingham) would do. He came towards her looking for the bird that he shot. When he looked down, Sarah was staring back up at him. Recognizing her from the posters, he picked her up and took her to a restaurant where she was cared for until an emergency helicopter arrived.

As Mark and Rhonda awoke Friday, they were filled with hope that Sarah would be found. They drove to the police station to undergo further questioning. While waiting in the hallway, Mark could hear cheering and excitement. He finally heard one lady say "I can't believe they found that little girl alive." He silently cried tears of joy and said a prayer of thanksgiving. "It happened just like we knew it would," Mark and Rhonda repeatedly said to each other.

Arriving at the hospital emergency room, Mark and Rhonda were reunited with their Sarah. She was being checked by the doctors; and samples of dirt, sticks from her hair, dried tears were being taken. She was scratched from head to toe and was dirty. "At first, she didn't look like our Sarah but we knew it was. She didn't respond to us at all," they recalled. She was in shock and did not say a word. "I guess I expected her to be the same as when

The elect are those individuals who shall find the Kingdom, because they came from it in the first place.

—Gospel of Thomas 49

*Your favorite doctrine,
Socrates, that knowledge is simply
recollection, if true, also neces-
sarily implies a previous time in
which we have learned that which
we now recollect. But this would
be impossible unless our soul had
been in some place before existing
in the form of man; here then is
another proof of the soul's
immortality.*

—Plato, "Phaedo,"
The Portable Plato

she was taken and say 'Hi Mom and Dad. Let's go home.' She had just been through a lot and was still trying to figure out what was happening."

Sarah just watched what was going on. Suddenly her countenance changed, and she smiled and said, "I saw Heather playing," referring to her desert companion. Heather is her younger sister. Mark and Rhonda did not understand at the time what that meant. They knew she could not have seen Heather because Heather was with them from the time Sarah was taken.

Sarah went right back into shock and didn't respond to any questions. It really didn't matter. Sarah was back! She spent the next day sleeping and gulping down food and drink. She did not say a word and did not smile.

The thing that impressed her most through the ordeal was that she saw a small child in the desert. Those were the first words she spoke.

It was finally Saturday morning that she started to talk. Sarah's account of the events of those four days was compiled and organized based on statements she made and questions asked her over the next month.

The Skidmores eventually returned to a semi-normal routine. Two more children soon arrived: Jessica and Ronald. When Jessica grew to be two or three years old, Sarah said that Jessica looked like the child in the desert. She had the same short, blond hair.

—The Skidmore Family

The Spirit existed before the flesh.

—The Apocryphon of James

Her Love Was Heavenly

Life is tremendously exciting when you are preparing to be married. I was engaged in April and had plans to tie the knot in July.

In May, I had an unexpected experience. During the night, about 1:00 A.M., I was awakened by a voice. It was a girl, standing by my bed. She was tall and lovely. I immediately knew she would be my first child. She said she loved me, and her love was heavenly. She expressed tremendous joy at the prospect of being able to come to Earth. It seemed that we already had a deep loving relationship—I had just forgotten. This experience lasted only a few moments.

Nycole was born a year and a half later. She is my love and the joy of my life. We are renewing our deep loving relationship.

—Karrie B.

A Cry in the Night

It was late one night in October of 1987. Our seven-year-old son was just home from the hospital after a serious injury. My husband and I were in the kitchen when we heard a child's voice cry, "Mommy, Daddy," several times. We ran to our children's room expecting to find one of them awake. They were all sound asleep. We returned to the kitchen.

About ten minutes later, we again heard a child's voice call out "Mommy, Daddy, please love me." We ran back to the room but again all of the children were sound asleep. Puzzled, we stood with the hall light on watching our sleeping children and trying to figure out where the voice had come from. And as we stood there watching them, the voice cried out again, "Mommy, Daddy, I want a hug." Suddenly, a warm peaceful feeling flooded into our souls as we knew that we were hearing a child needing to come to our family. Maybe the timing was diffi-

MOTHER TELL ME A STORY

Child: Mother tell me the story
*   that I love to hear*
Tell me of Heaven and why I
*   came here.*
Mother tell how you love me and
*   gently speak,*
And then I'll go to sleep.

Mother: Child, I am here,
Can you feel that Heaven is
*   near—*
Sleep, sleep, a lovewatch I'll
*   keep,*
To protect you through the night.

Child: Tell me how you love me
*   and gently speak,*
And then I'll go to sleep.

Mother: Sleep, sleep, a lovewatch
*   I'll keep,*
To protect you through the night.

—Janice Kapp Perry

cult because of our son's injury and long recovery ahead, but we would not turn that sweet spirit away.

Now, four years later, my eyes fill with tears when our precious son says to us, "Mommy, Daddy, I love you and I want a hug." In his unique, special voice we again hear the cry in the night and his great need for our love and acceptance.

—Debbie C.

A Father's Letter

The following was written by my father after I had my experience with my unborn child.

—Lisa D.

Dear Daughter,

Early this morning while driving, my thoughts centered upon you and your new baby. Some very strong, spiritual feelings came to me:

This child comes to you as a special gift from God. She comes to you in the form of a blessing and a healing influence. She is different from the other children, not only in gender, but in her temperament and feelings. She is a choice spirit—one who was chosen to come forth at this particular time for a specific purpose. She has the special gift to love others unconditionally, and she will enlarge the capacity of many, including you, her mother, to love as the Savior loved.

Emmy, as she will be known, will greatly bless your life for good. She will strengthen your heart and spirit, and she will help to strengthen your conviction of the gospel. She will soothe and soften your heart and disposition, and help you to better understand and appreciate your mission in life.

She will be very close to your heart, bonding with you in a very unique, eternal way. She will fill a seemingly empty spot in your heart and soul, that heretofore seemed unfulfilled. Because of your special closeness to one another, she will seem, at times, to be more of a companion and sister to you than a daughter. And yet, she will be a wonderful daughter who will require the close, delicate, deliberate teachings of a devoted mother.

You were very close to her before you were born, and you both knew that you would be privileged to live as mother and daughter in mortality. You experienced great anticipation in awaiting the time when you would come to earth together in a close family setting. You were blessed to see her in vision before she was born, and as you know, she was seen with you in vision, many years ago by your father.

How is my Father, the Father of Light? How is my Mother, the Mother of the Living, whom I left, and her brethren also? Rejoice with me, ye Holy Ones, for I have returned to my original state again, my archaic, my original ruler, and place.

—Allberry,
Manichaean Psalm-Book,
2:197-99

Emmy will be blessed with many gifts of the Spirit throughout her life. She will not know of her gifts at first, and will need to be helped to recognize and appreciate them. These special gifts are given to help others find the truth, and to glorify God.

Be assured that your Savior and Friend walks closely with you, especially during those times when you feel all alone. He stands over you in those special times of need, trying to manifest Himself to you, to help you and assist you in your trials and tribulations. There are many times when, if you would but look up, prayerfully, with a simple faith, you would see Him, and He would minister unto you. You are never alone, and never without someone by your side who loves you, though unseen they may be. Seek to know this, and seek to use this blessing for yourself, and for those who have been given to you.

I pray that you may come to know and understand the truth of all things, and that you may fulfill the true measure of your creation, as an individual, as a wife, and as a mother. For you too, like your daughter, are a special daughter of our Heavenly Father, endowed with special gifts and blessings from your heavenly home. May God bless you always.

Your loving father and eternal friend.

Happy those early days, when I
Shin'd in my Angel-Infancy!
Before I understood this place
Appointed for my second race,
Or taught my soul to fancy aught
But a white celestial thought:
When yet I had not walk'd above
A mile or two from my first Love,
And looking back—at that short
  space—
Could see a glimpse of His bright
  face.

—Henry Vaughn
"The Retreat"
The Complete Poetry of
Henry Vaughn

My Three Year Old Knew Before I Did

My three year old awoke one morning and told me how we will be taking a little baby brother to her older brother's "Tee Ball" games during the following summer. I was not aware of even a possibility of pregnancy as not one of my menstrual cycles had been missed. I immediately obtained a pregnancy test, which verified that I was indeed pregnant.

—*Carol E.*[1]

The Nearness of My Unborn Children

The reality of life before life was brought to my attention through a series of experiences with my unborn children.

My family and I were attending our niece's baby blessing at her church. During this spiritual meeting I saw two spirit-children sitting on the row in front of us. They appeared to be around eight years of age: a boy and a girl. Since it was my niece's first baby, I thought I was seeing her other children that were to come to her. Just as I was thinking this, a voice told me, "No, these are your children." I was very excited, as it has been difficult for me to get pregnant. And it turned out that I had conceived just before this experience occurred.

I was three and one-half months pregnant when I

*I wish I could remember
The days before my birth
And if I knew the Father
Before I came to earth.
In quiet moments when I'm all
    alone
I close my eyes and try to see my
Heavenly Home.*

—Janice Kapp Perry

suffered a traumatic miscarriage. I wondered why I had to go through all this when it had been made known to me that I was going to have these children. Would I still have these children? Had the miscarriage changed that? Was there a reason I had miscarried? All the questions people ask themselves at such difficult times went through my mind.

In a dream that night, my deceased grandfather brought two spirit children to me. I do not know how to explain where we were, but they came down a path that led to a small rock bench like one might see in a park. They were holding hands and excited because it was getting close to the time they could come to earth. My grandfather was helping to prepare them for this earthly experience. They told me that they needed perfect bodies and minds in order to fill their missions on earth. That is why I had the miscarriage. They were still mine and would still be coming to me.

From this experience, I gained the realization that I had this miscarriage because several weeks earlier I had gotten sick from carbon monoxide. We had recently driven in a car that we did not realize had exhaust problems. The carbon monoxide would have crossed the placenta, and most likely have damaged the brain of my unborn child.

In another special vision or dream I found myself in the pre-earthly existence walking along with my daughter. She and I were both grown women and the best of friends. She was talking to me about her worries of coming to earth and living so she could come back here. We both knew I was to be her mother and that is why she was talking to me about her concerns. She stopped and looked at me and said, "Help me get back to Father."

We have a special responsibility as parents to teach our children, to be the examples they need, so they can go back to live with Father.

Another night, I woke up suddenly with the feeling that someone was watching me. I thought it must be one of my children who had awakened in the night, standing by my bed. As I turned over and looked, it was a beautiful little girl. She was wearing a long, white dress with long sleeves and an empire style waist. Her hair was pulled back in a pony tail. I remember her face and the shape of her nose. She was so pretty, I wanted to hold her. I reached out to touch her, but she was gone. I was pregnant at the time and wondered if she was the baby I was carrying. She let me know somehow that she was there to see how I was. She was concerned for me.

There are three groups of people living in every village. First are those you can see—walking around, eating, sleeping, and working. Second are the ancestors, whom Grandma Yaisa had now joined. And the third people are those waiting to be born.

—Alex Haley, Roots (New York: Doubleday, 1976), p.18.

When the baby was born, it was another boy. This little boy was a bonus baby in addition to the two I had seen in my vision. I was grateful to receive this dear little child. Less than two years later I was blessed with a baby daughter. I knew it was the little spirit who had shown her love and compassion that night several years earlier. She had the face and nose that I remembered, and she still has the same gift of love and concern for me and others that she had before she came to this earth.

When I was about eight months pregnant with her, I was very close to death because of heart problems that were worsened by pregnancy. I was awakened in the night by someone saying, "Mother." I turned over, and there was a tall, slender boy spirit calling me "mother". I knew this meant I was to be his mother also, and my reaction was to yell, "No!" I knew I had hurt his feelings as he immediately turned and left. I climbed out of bed and got on my knees and told the Lord that I did not mean to hurt him, but I did not know if I could even live through this pregnancy. It had been so hard, and now I was in my last month and knew I had harder times to face. I did not know if I could do it again. But, I told the Lord that if he would help me again, I would do it.

I thought I would wait a few years to help me

I cannot tell my story without reaching a long way back. If it were possible I would reach back farther still—into the very first years of my childhood, and beyond them into distant ancestral past...

—Hermann Hesse, Demian

regain some of my health, but I was shocked to find I was pregnant after four months. We thought we had been careful not to let this happen.

I will try to describe some of the things I learned and endured with this next pregnancy. It was very hard, but the Lord was true to his word and helped me through it. With a small family and a baby to take care of besides the pregnancy and heart problems, I would go to bed at night exhausted. Some nights I was so weak, I would lay in bed and cry because it seemed that if I went to sleep I would die because I did not have the strength to live through the night. I would lay in bed and pray, and tell the Lord that unless he helped me, I would die. Each time this happened, my grandfather who had died several years earlier, would walk into my bedroom and tell me I could go to sleep and everything would be okay. I was also aware of others who would come to help me. One night I woke up and could see through the walls into my kitchen where there was a whole group of people who were there just to take care of me. They were medical people and concerned loved ones. I was told that they were close by so they could be there when I needed them.

When I was only a couple of weeks from delivery of our last child, I was having a dream, when suddenly a

That is why every man's story is important, eternal, sacred...In each individual the spirit has become flesh...

—Hermann Hesse, Demian

little baby face appeared to me, stopping my dream. He appeared very tiny: younger than newborn. He was crying, and I could not comfort him. I kept asking him what was wrong. He finally told me that he was hurting. At that I woke up. I knew it was my unborn child telling me that something was wrong. I immediately got out of bed and started to pray, asking the Lord to help my child. That day my husband and brother gave me a blessing by the laying on of hands, and I was told that the baby would be protected, that he would be born healthy, and that I would know when he was born what the problem had been. When he was born, the cord was around his neck, causing problems with birth, but he was protected and healthy as I had been blessed.

I am so grateful to the Lord for these mighty blessings and for his mercy in allowing me to bring these precious children into our home.

—*Laura D.*

My hour is come; they summon me. I will go from your midst and return to my true home.

—Allberry
Manichaean Psalm-Book, 2:72

Triplets Foreshadowed

I had thought my child-bearing years were passed, for I was well into my forties. I dreamed I was giving birth, and then saw myself holding three beautiful babies. Within a year I had given birth to a sweet and precious baby girl, and my married daughter gave birth to her firstborn, a son; followed shortly by my daughter-in-law who had her third baby, a boy. Indeed, I did hold in my arms three beautiful babies, all mine...my own infant daughter and two infant grandsons.

—*Carol E.*[2]

Asked of God

After having ten children, I received much pressure to limit my family. I knew these concerns stemmed from worry and love for me. I wondered if perhaps I had sufficiently fulfilled the law of increase. However, I wanted my Heavenly Father's stamp of approval.

In prayer and fasting I knelt before him and asked if there was a child yet waiting to come to our family. In a seeming split second, I beheld a beautiful garden and a marble-like bench. On the bench was seated a fully-grown personage with the saddest countenance I had ever seen. Not a word was spoken, but the message was clear, and it burned within my heart. This spirit was saddened because I was considering ending childbearing. He wanted to be part of our family, and it was his time to come to this mortal state. How could I say no. Twelve months later we were blessed with our eleventh child, whom we named Samuel, which means "asked of God."

To our joy and surprise, sixteen months later, I was to give birth to yet another beautiful son. In a blessing by the laying on of hands, I was told that the Lord loved me, had accepted my sacrifice, and was pleased with me for fulfilling covenants made in my pre-earth life by having these children—while many were refusing to let these children enter their homes. I was told that the Lord had chosen to add to our happiness a very special child. With great satisfaction and supreme joy we welcomed Joseph, which means, "he shall add" to our family.

—*Carol E.*[3]

I came forth from the Father, and am come into the world; again I leave the world and go to the Father.

—*John 16:28*

I Was Not Alone in My Car

When I was thirty, I had a special experience. I was a mother of four sons ranging in age from two to eight. My husband was a school teacher, and we were living on his income alone. I worked diligently being a Mom and homemaker. I had absolutely *no* desire to have any more children. I did not feel that I could handle it emotionally or financially.

Soon I had reason to believe that I might be pregnant again. I was very scared and upset.

I play racquetball often, and one Summer evening I was driving home after a game. Alone in my car, I noticed that it was an exceptionally beautiful evening: the temperature was perfect. The sun was just setting over the Great Salt Lake. Suddenly, I got an overwhelming feeling that I was not alone in my car. I *felt* someone there, but no words were spoken out loud. I had never felt anything like that before. I felt calm.

I just *knew* this spirit person who was there with me was my unborn child. This person was communicating with me through my feelings. The spirit being told me that I did not need to worry, that I would indeed have a baby, and that it would be a positive and good thing. This left me feeling calm and happy. I knew that everything would be all right.

When I was about seven months pregnant, I was feeling overwhelmed and tired as I was getting closer to having another addition to our already large family. I was extremely worried that I was going to have another "wild" boy. I already had four of them, and I assumed that I would probably have another one.

One night while I was sleeping, I was dreaming like normal. The next thing I knew I was somewhere else. It was like when you are watching television and someone switches channels with the remote control. I was in the middle of a circle of people. I could not see their faces but I could feel that I had no reason to be afraid. They felt somewhat familiar. I could see that they had something to show me. They were together holding a baby girl, and she was crying. I noticed she had a strong and healthy cry. She looked to be about five or six months

We living men and women, while associated with this mortal organism, are ignorant of whatever experience our larger selves may have gone through in the past—yet when we wake out of this present materialized condition, we may gradually realize...the wide range of knowledge which that larger entity must have accumulated since its intelligence and memory began.

—Sir Oliver Lodge
Science and Immortality

old and was wearing a red plaid dress. Her face and eyes stuck in my mind—especially her eyes. The people held her out to me and put her in my arms. I was overcome with joy when she was placed in my arms. I questioned them. "This is *my* baby?" No words were spoken, but I knew what they were telling me. When I looked down at her I *knew* that she was mine. Then I woke up and sat up in bed. I knew that this had been more than a dream. I had feelings that I had never before experienced.

On April 28, 1991, I gave birth to my baby girl. As soon as she was born, the doctor laid her on my stomach and her little eyes were looking at me. Her face was very familiar to me. I knew those eyes. I recognized her as the baby in my dream.

—*Lisa D.*

Ye are gods; and all of you are children of the Most High.

—*Psalm 82:6*

My Husband Was With Our Unborn Grandchild

In December, 1983, I was in Texas visiting my parents, and my daughter was in Hawaii expecting her second child. I was notified that labor had begun earlier than expected for my daughter. Feeling the need to sort things out, I went for a walk.

While pondering, I saw a picture in my mind of my husband who had died sixteen years earlier. He was smiling happily and standing beside a lovely, dark-haired girl. I knew this was our soon-to-be grand-daughter, and I felt assured that all would be well. Time proved this to be true.

—Ann H.

My Unborn Son

One evening, years ago, my wife and I sat alone together in the playroom of our house. The children were all asleep in their beds, and we were waiting for the birth of a new little baby. My wife, big with child, was sitting by the table. We were talking softly together, knowing that the baby would arrive that night. The lights were low, and there was a feeling of love for each other and for the baby that was to come. I remember looking at my wife— she was rocking quietly, her eyes closed, her pale white hands spread across her full waist. The sweet feeling in the room grew and persisted. It was very powerful. I said to her, "Do you feel this all around us?" and she replied, "Yes." It was lovely being with her there then. It was a sweet closeness, a unity I can hardly describe.

"Can you tell?" I said. "We shall have a son."

"I know," she replied. "It will be a boy."

And then for me the veil parted, and I saw our

*When my
bones were
being formed,
carefully
put together
in my mother's womb,
when I was
growing there
in secret,
You knew that
I was there—
You saw me before
I was born.
The days allotted
to me had all
been recorded
in Your book,
before any
of them
ever began.*

*—Psalm 139:15-16
Life Educational Corp.
Tempe, Arizona*

son, standing, waiting, a few feet from the chair my wife was rocking in. He was tall and well-formed, taller and larger, it seemed to me, than the room allowed. There was power about his person, great power and goodness and patience and love.

I said, "Do you see him there standing beside you?"

Again there swelled that sweet feeling of closeness and unity. She looked at me, confident, a small smile on her lips. "I don't need to," she said. "I know he is there."

—Richard G. Ellsworth[4]

Dream Boy in the Garden

The moment I saw my little boy, I fell completely in love with him. He was so adorable with his blonde hair curling about his angelic little face. I remember so clearly how it felt to look into those pure little eyes and experience this gaze of such incredible wisdom. The desire to pick him up and enfold his little body in my arms and hug him to me grew in my heart. There and then we forged a bond which I knew would last forever. Then he continued on with his play and danced out of sight across the beautiful meadow, leaving me to wonder if I was awake or asleep?

As I lay in my bed half awake, half asleep, my mind contemplated the vision I had just experienced: the scene of the lovely garden from which emanated feelings of peaceful happiness. The very flowers and grasses swayed in harmony, as if blown by a gentle breeze filled with soft music. Into this peaceful scene, the figure of a little child came dancing, as though from off the wings of a theater stage. Although he was moving quickly, his movements were in total harmony with his surroundings. He seemed completely comfortable there. He continued to play and dance, softly laughing as children do when they are totally absorbed with their amusements.

I watched, fascinated at the beautiful picture I was observing. The child moved closer to me, and I could see that it was a little boy with fair hair. The breeze would catch little tufts of his hair and move them slightly as he ran back and forth across the garden. Then, when he was quite close to me, he stopped and looked at me, and that was when our eyes met. And though he never spoke, we had a complete understanding of the love that passed between us.

The Spirit itself beareth witness with our spirit, that we are the children of God.

—Romans 8:16

Now into my mind came thoughts that were so clearly defined that there could be no confusion. This little boy was an unborn child that was waiting for his turn to come into this world. I was to be his mother, and it was my responsibility to see that he did not have to wait much longer. When he was born I was to name him Andrew, because his name had already been chosen.

Having basked in the splendor of this vision I had been privileged to experience, I then remembered some grim realities. We already had seven children, and my husband had, only a few days before, made it very clear that our family was complete and that there would be no more children. I had agreed, even though those little stirrings of maternal love had been tugging at me.

The other problem was much more acute. To my sorrow, a rift was growing between my husband and I. He was working later in the evenings, and his extra activities took him away more and more from the family. My life was filled with the daily chores that accompany a large family and life on a farm in Australia. We were also very active in church and community affairs. So there was not too much time for self pity.

This did not seem to be an ideal time to tell my husband about my dream or to express the desire that we have another child. So I kept these things to myself and wondered what I could do to see that beautiful little boy that I knew was waiting to come to me.

There was only one time that whole month that we were intimate enough to conceive a child. But the miracle happened, and I was pregnant. It was a difficult pregnancy, and there were even times when I feared that I would miscarry. The last three months, I was confined to bed and could hardly walk because of a separated pelvis. Yet

God that made the world...hath made of one blood all nations of men for to dwell on all the face of the earth: and hath determined the times before appointed and the bounds of their habitations.

—Acts 17: 24, 26

despite the problems, I delivered a healthy baby boy, and I was allowed to name him Andrew.

When Andrew was six weeks old, my husband sent the eight children and myself on a cruise through the South Pacific to America. He accompanied us to Fiji, then flew back to Australia, because he could not leave his business affairs longer than the week he had spent on the ship. We continued on and disembarked in Los Angeles, where friends met us and got us settled for the night. We had a great time seeing the sights and visiting Disneyland and all the attractions to which the children had been looking forward.

During the month that followed, I did not think about my dream of Andrew because my life was filled with events that used up all my thoughts and energies. My husband deserted us and left us to sort out our own lives, because he was busy building a life with another woman. The story of our survival is a miracle in itself.

The children and I ended up living in Utah, and I eventually remarried. My new husband adopted all of the eight children, and we settled down to a wonderful life in Salt Lake City.

One lovely, Spring day, I was looking out the large picture window, which overlooked the lawn in the back

For as thou hast not forgotten the people who now are and those who have passed away, so I remember those who are appointed to come.

—The Apocalypse of Baruch

yard. Andrew was playing by himself in the grass—happy in the warm sunshine. He was about three years old with blonde hair and blue eyes. He stopped for a moment when he saw me looking at him, and our eyes met through the glass. I saw a look of pure happy love in his eyes. Instantly the dream that I had before he was born came to my mind, and I recognized the identical child from that beautiful garden in my dream.

Someone, somewhere knew that events in my life were taking such a turn that Andrew had to come then, or who knows when....

—Jean H.

Babies are bits of star-dust blown from the hand of God. Lucky the woman who knows the pangs of birth for she has held a star.

—Larry Barretto,
The Indiscreet Years

Prophecy Fulfilled

My nephew was jabbering to me while I was fixing my hair in the bathroom. He was barely three, yet quite verbal. I had two children at the time. His conversation went something like the following: "You know you will need five more beds in your house, because you are going to have five more kids. Now they are in heaven, and they are big. They are nice. They have teeth now, but when they are born they won't have any." Interestingly, four of those five are now here.

—*Carol E.*[5]

A Part of Our Family

Before our eighth child, I knew there was a little somebody who wanted to be part of our family. I felt it as a shadow following me around. I fretted over it. I had *no* desire to go through the health problems I had faced with the last three births—each a little more difficult—or the work that came afterwards. I did not know what to do. I was not sure I could handle another baby.

One night I dreamt I was very large with child. In my dream I put my hand on my tummy and felt the baby kick within. Love filled my heart till I felt it would burst for that little spirit. I woke knowing I wanted that little spirit to join our family.

From these experiences, it seemed I already knew Mary Ann, and I wanted to do all I could to help her join our family. I prepared myself physically by walking early every morning and eating wisely. Heavenly Father blessed us with her the following year. Caring for this little girl I loved before was a joy and not work after all.

—Kathy S.

God one morning, glad of heaven,
  Laughed—and that was you!

        —Brian Hooker from
        "A Little Person"
        (Babies p. 21)

He Was Excited to Come

Growing up in a large family, I was resentful at times when a new member of the family would come along. Because of our financial situation, I did not think it was wise for Mom and Dad to have more children.

In 1984 while at a college game in Pittsburgh, I met my Uncle and Aunt from South Carolina. They had come up to see their Alma Mater play against the Panthers.

My aunt was expecting at the time and commented that there was a rumor that my mother was also expecting. I was not too excited about this. Eleven children!

On my way home, I sat in the back seat. We had exhausted all of the excitement from the game. During this time of peace, I offered a silent prayer. I asked God if my mother was pregnant.

Within a few moments, I was overcome with a

tremendous love and peace. I actually felt a spirit come and sit next to me in the back seat of the car. He told me: "Yes, Mom is expecting. I am your brother and love you very much." He was excited to come.

All my resentment was gone. He had just as much right as I to experience life. I wonder what Mom thought when she read my next letter, in which I told her the baby would be a boy.

—*Karrie B.*

THROUGH THE VEIL

"Look, Grandpa,
can you see her there—
My mother down below?"

"Yes, dear one,
She's so much like you
She'll love you; help you grow.

"I miss her!
Will you tell her that?
Then both of you will know."

—*Barbara G. Dykstra*
Copyright © 1993
(Used by Permission)

Love at First Sight

The conception of our fourth child was a difficult time. We had just moved to Mesa, Arizona. My husband had gone into a partnership with my brother, whose business was already falling apart. I got pregnant almost immediately upon arriving. We had no medical insurance, and shortly after, we had no job as the business went under.

We were living in a tiny two bedroom apartment with three children. I wondered how I would ever be able to care for another child. I did not want to be pregnant and often times felt that my body had been invaded. Many nights I cried about my situation, not wanting this baby and yet feeling guilty because I was a mommy and should love all my children.

One night when I was about six months pregnant, I went to bed feeling hateful towards my unborn baby. I

Forasmuch then as we are the offspring of God...

—The Acts 17:29

dreamed that I could look down into my womb and when I did I saw the face of the most beautiful, dark-haired, round-faced baby. He spoke to me and said, "It's all right, Mommy, because I love you." Unfortunately this dream did not comfort me. I made an appointment with our church leader for some counseling. When I told him of all the emotions I was going through with this pregnancy, he promised me that when they laid him in my arms after his birth it would be love at first sight.

The time eventually came for him to be born. While I was in labor he developed a prolapsed cord and had to be born Cesarean section. I had general anesthesia and was not aware of his birth. My husband brought our new son into my recovery room and asked me if I wanted to see him. I said, "No, not really." He said, "But he's really cute." So I held him for the first time. As Nathan was laid in my arms and I looked into the very same face I had seen in my dream it was instant love. To this day, that eight-year-old boy has a very special place in my heart.

Our next child was a surprise also. One night while I was waiting in our living room for the rest of the family to join me for family prayer, I saw a little girl about two or three with dark brown hair run past the doorway in the other room. I got up to see who it was. There was no one there. When my husband came into the living room, I told him what I had seen. He looked up into heaven and said, "Sarah, we're not ready for you yet."

Nathan was only a year at the time. We had just moved into a bigger house and were just barely getting our feet under us. A baby at that time just was not in our plans. However, within the month I was pregnant again. On rare occasions I would hear the sound of a child almost laughing. I knew this pregnancy would be different as I was not going to let myself suffer the guilt of an unwanted baby. So I immediately accepted my condition and felt excited about the prospects of a little sister for our only daughter, who informed us that if I had one more boy she was moving out. About two months into the pregnancy I started to miscarry, which would have been the "perfect solution" to an unplanned pregnancy. To my surprise, I really wanted this little person. So I spent the next four months in bed. Ultrasound revealed that we were to have another boy. How could this be? Had I not seen a little girl? Andrew made his entrance into this world too soon. He was born twelve weeks early and weighed just under three pounds. We prayed over him constantly to get bigger and stronger, and to please

Whence comest thou? Thine origin? What art thou doing here? ...Knowest thou not that thou art a spark of Deity, struck from the fire of His eternal blaze, and brought forth in the midst of eternal burning?

Knowest thou not that eternities ago thy spirit, pure and holy, dwelt in thy Heavenly Father's bosom and in His presence, and with thy mother, one of the queens of heaven, surrounded by they brother and sister spirits in the spirit world, among the Gods?

—John Taylor

come home. My arms ached to hold him and to be his mommy. One day we went to his little bed in the hospital and told him that we wanted him to get well and come home, but if Heavenly Father needed him more it was alright with us for him to go to Him. That was so hard to do, for I thought that he would die, but to our surprise from that moment on he started making progress.

For many years I wondered why I had seen this little girl in the other room. I thought maybe we would adopt her, or maybe she would come to our family some other time or way. After Andrew I felt it was too risky to have another child and I was not going to get pregnant. One morning I got up to use some contraceptive and heard an audible voice say, "If you want your little girl, do not use that." I put it down and told my husband what I had just heard. We decided that we would trust the Lord and have another baby.

I started with the same problems as I did Andrew and was extra careful this time. Sarah was born on time; a big, healthy, baby. The only conclusion that we could come to as to why Andrew was born before Sarah is when my husband looked up into heaven that night and told her we were not ready for her she told Andrew to go instead.

Thus saith the Lord, thy Redeemer, and He that formed thee from the womb, I am the Lord that maketh all things; that stretcheth forth the heavens alone; that spreadeth abroad the earth by myself;

—*Isaiah 44:24*

Though some of our babies came as surprises and not especially wanted in the beginning, each one has brought a uniqueness to our family. Each has been a great joy in our home.

—Betsy L.

When I was born, I drew in the common air, and fell upon the earth...
and the first voice which I uttered was crying, as all others do....
For there is no king that had any other beginning of birth...
all men have one entrance into life, and the like going out.

—Wisdom of Solomon
(Babies, p. 23)

My Golden Warrior

My husband and I were married on a beautiful Spring day. The sun was shining, and we felt as if all of the earth was celebrating the beginning of our marriage. That day, in privacy, we promised each other and the Lord that we would accept children according to his will.

I had a four-year scholarship, and we had very little money. My husband also had many years of schooling left. So of course, the rational thing to do would be to wait a few years before having children. We had things figured out so logically and carefully.

Then one calm, peaceful night during our evening prayers, we had the feeling that a little one was supposed to come to our home now. We did not want to begin our family this soon. We fought these feelings and their implications, and even began choosing not to pray, because we knew those same feelings would come. After a tremendous struggle, we decided that we must keep our covenant with our Savior. We decided we had to trust him to know what was right for us and our baby.

As soon as we accepted this decision, joy filled our hearts and souls. During the months that followed, we had many dreams about our son. We learned through the Spirit what his name was to be, that he would be a warrior for the Lord's work, and that he would have a golden, beautiful face. We saw his beautiful, curious eyes many times in our dreams. We received the knowledge that if we had refused to accept him now, he would have been sent to another family. How humble this made us feel. How close we came to losing that blessing.

When he was born, his beautiful eyes looked around carefully. Many nurses commented on the fact that he did not fall asleep for several hours after he was born. And in my heart, I was and will ever be grateful that we accepted our little golden warrior.

—*Debbie C.*

GOLDEN WARRIOR

So wide awake,
So newly born,
So nearly missed
Our warrior son.

—Barbara G. Dykstra
Copyright © 1993
(Used by Permission)

My Angel Wrapped in Light

I was five and one-half months pregnant with my third child. The doctors discovered gall stones blocking the liver and pancreas duct. Doing immediate surgery, they saved my life and that of the baby. The surgery took many hours and was very difficult. I bled heavily, and for a few seconds my heart stopped. My husband was told that there was little chance that the baby would survive.

One difficult night the nurse was performing the routine check of the baby's heartbeat. She could not find it. She checked for over a half of an hour and finally called a nurse and doctor from the maternity floor. They checked for over an hour. I was told that they felt the baby had died and started to set up an ultrasound to verify it. They left to call my husband and doctor.

Alone in a darkened room, I poured out my heart to

ANGEL CHILD

Eyes of clearest, crystal blue,
Hair as black as night,
Smiling cherub given me
All wrapped in heaven's light.

"My little sister, much beloved.
Raise her," the Savior said,
"Teach her; help her find the
    way;
Walk paths that I have tread."

Then down the heavenly stair I
    came.
Awakened to earth's sight
Knowing I would hold her soon—
My angel wrapped in light.

—*Barbara G. Dykstra*
Copyright © 1993
(Used by Permission)

the Lord. My heart grieved for the baby I had never held, the smiles I had never seen, the steps never carefully counted. As I pleaded with the Lord for strength to accept it and peace for my spirit, I fell into a deep sleep.

I dreamt that I was at the bottom of a flight of white steps. Around me were my husband, my two sons, my parents, sister and brother, and departed loved ones. I heard my name called and looked up to the top of the staircase. There was a throne surrounded by a light and a figure standing before the throne. A feeling of great love, compassion, warmth and calmness entered my spirit. I began climbing the stairs and knelt on the stair below his feet. I bowed my head in reverence and awe. Suddenly hands descended into my view. In these beautiful hands rested a glowing baby wrapped in white. I gazed into crystal blue eyes with beautiful black lashes. She had dark black hair, and as I gazed, she smiled at me. I began to cry from joy and amazement.

Then I heard these words, "I give this child to you to raise for me. She is a gift that someday you will return to me. She is my little sister and is very beloved. Teach her of my love. Show her my example. Help her find me and my path. I died for her and for the chance to bring her back to Father. Behold, the precious gift I give to you."

The light grew and suddenly I knew her. I received glimpses of long ago and promises made. I yearned to keep those promises and to hold my precious gift.

The bundle was placed in my hands, and my tears dropped to the white blanket. I felt awed and amazed at this great trust in me. How could I ever be worthy of this beautiful gift? I slowly walked down the stairs and stood before my husband. I held out my arms, and he gently took the angel of light from me.

I suddenly woke up when the doctor returned. I told him to check the baby again, because I knew she was alive and strong. He agreed, and on his first try found a strong, regular heartbeat.

Three months later I gave birth to a seven pound, six ounce baby girl. She had crystal blue eyes, dark black hair and looked exactly like the baby in my dream. And as I gazed into her eyes, I saw again the angel wrapped in light.

—Debbie C.

"The child comes from somewhere else... (and) there is a constant coming or going between us and the world of the ancestors...Then it's the child who can tell you about that world since its coming from there—it's not the old man who's going there but the child who's coming from there."

—Jonathan Cott
"Chinua Achebe: At The Crossroads—An Interview with the Nigerian Writer," Parabola— Myth and the Quest for Meaning

I'm Ready to Come Now

I was expecting our third baby. My husband was applying for internships to Washington, D.C. and New York in order to complete his requirements to graduate in Journalism. If he got an internship, he would be away from April through August. The baby would be due at the same time. We had to make the decision of either forfeiting the internship and postponing graduation, or having me stay home. We prayed and worried about what we should do, willing to sacrifice whatever for the Lord.

Eight weeks into the pregnancy I began to bleed. Although I stayed in bed the next six weeks to try to save the baby, I miscarried what would have been a little boy. My husband did get the internship and I accompanied him.

In August, the week before we returned home, I

dreamt of a little blond, blue-eyed boy standing in white looking at me and saying, "I'm ready to come *now*." Joseph was born the following spring.

The way Joseph had said, "Now" in this dream gave me the distinct impression at the time that he had allowed my husband and I to have this opportunity in the East that changed our lives. This important episode of our life was something we had to experience together. Ultimately, it steered us towards an eight-year opportunity of service and growth in Virginia. We could not have had this opportunity if Paul had been alone for the internship or had postponed graduation. Still today, Joseph has the most giving personality.

—*Kathy S.*

And let us face it: 'deep down' nobody in his right mind can visualize his own existence without assuming that he has always lived and will live hereafter; and the religious world-views of old only endowed this psychological instinct with images which could be shared, transmitted, and ritualized.

—*Eric Erikson*
Gandhi's Truth

Tell Me About Grandpa Robert

I was putting three-year-old Johnny to bed when he asked for a bedtime story. For the past few weeks I had been telling him of the adventures of his great-great-grandfather: a colonizer, a soldier, a community leader. As I started another story, Johnny stopped me and said, "No, tell me of Grandpa Robert." I was surprised. This was *my* grandpa. I had not told stories of him, and I could not imagine where he had heard his name. He had died before I had even married.

"How do you know about Grandpa Robert?" I asked.

"Well, mamma," he said with reverence, "he's the one who brought me to earth."

—*Lois P.*

I Was the Baby
of Her Dreams

When I was small, my parents told me of the circumstances of my birth. They were a young couple living on a limited income and difficult circumstances. He worked hard raising wheat. She worked hard raising children. When the youngest child was several months old, my mother became pregnant and then miscarried. They were physically and emotionally exhausted. Recuperation was not easy. The doctor warned Mom against doing all the things that are demanded of a mother of a young family, so my dad carried as much household and family work as he could. It was a time of struggle and courage.

After several months, she became pregnant again. Life continued to be extremely difficult. During this pregnancy she had a comforting dream. In the dream, she said she saw "a beautiful baby: a very special and precious baby."

Then I was born—healthy and "as red as a beet." A few months later, a friend of the family gave us some hand-me-down children's clothes. Included in these clothes was a white ruffled baby bonnet. Mother put the bonnet on me, and there I was, the baby of her dream.

I shall be eternally grateful to my good parents who, in a time of difficulty, welcomed me into their home and into their hearts. I am truly blessed.

—*Taffy*

Thou hast chosen him you loved in the spirit world to be thy companion...All these were arranged, likewise the spirits that should tabernacle through your lineage.

—*John Taylor*

A Visit by My Daughter

This is a story that I hold near my heart, one that changed my life and that of my family. In 1986, I came home from the hospital with Porter, my fourth boy, having the feeling that our family was complete. I was twenty-eight years old, and excited to be finished having babies before I had reached thirty. My husband was an electrician, and our boys ranged in age from seven to the newborn. We lived in a home and area that I loved.

Just after we brought our new baby home from the hospital, I started hearing the cry of babies. I would rush to Porter's room, thinking it was him, only to find him sleeping peacefully. I have always been the kind of mother that would rather hold my babies and let the laundry sit and the dust collect than to let them cry with needs unmet. This went on for three months, making me wonder if maybe I wasn't going crazy.

I told my husband, Michael, about these occurrences, and he remarked that maybe we were supposed to have more kids. At that point in my life, that was absolutely the last thing I wanted to think about! I felt overwhelmed with our boys. I was home-schooling the two older boys, and I was supplementing our income with an early morning paper-route. I always felt bone-tired because I got up at 2:00 a.m. seven days a week for my route—on top of being a wife and homemaker. Somewhere in the back of my mind, I knew Michael could be right, but I would not bring myself to pray about that. Instead, I pleaded with Heavenly Father in prayer, that the crying would go away. Within days it stopped and I felt relieved and even let it slip from my mind altogether.

About six months later, I started to hear the crying again. I was still nursing Porter and would often lay in bed at night with him beside me, knowing that the other boys were snuggled soundly in bed, yet I was listening to the sound of a crying baby. That is when I began wondering why this was happening and if there was a message there for me.

Often, I receive answers to prayers and personal revelation even when busy around the house caring for

As the eye of man reaches the stars where it had its primitive origin, so the soul penetrated and sees even within the divine state of being wherein he lives.

—Jacob Boehme
The Doctrine of Jacob Boehme

my family. I probably pray more while vacuuming or doing the dishes than on my knees beside my bed. But what happened that spring day took me by surprise.

I was alone in the kitchen, cleaning the stove. The three older boys were outside playing, and Porter was asleep on my bed. The house was quiet and peaceful. I was feeling content with my life, when suddenly I heard, "Mommy, Mommy!" I turned around, still knowing that everyone else was outside. To my great astonishment, six feet from me I beheld a little girl about five years old! I could see her perfectly clear, yet I was also aware that she was a spirit and not of flesh and blood. She was wearing a white ruffly pinafore and dress with shoulder-length hair. I knew immediately that this little girl was to be our daughter.

"My goodness! Her hair is so dark," I thought. Our boys were strawberry blonds, and both Michael's family and mine have mostly fair skin and hair. I did not move toward her, we just stood looking into each other's eyes. Although I had heard her with my ears when she first called me, we did not speak vocally again but communicated spirit to spirit. I knew what she was thinking, and she would answer my thoughts. I learned so much in the seconds that followed—and they were seconds, but it

FEARFULLY AND WONDERFULLY MADE

For I am fearfully and wonderfully made.
Knit together inside of your womb.
God knew me before my body was formed.
He loved me before time was born.

—Cynthia Lynn (Martin) Morgan, Mt. Moriah Music, St. Paul, MN, 1992. Used by Permission.

seemed like such a long time. The thoughts would come to my mind, and I recognized them as truth.

She was most anxious to come to earth—and so excited about letting me know this. She loved the boys and knew Michael and I well from our pre-earth life. I also learned that we had all chosen to be together on Earth and that she was anxious to join us. She told me that she knew I was trying to create an atmosphere that would invite God's spirit into our home, and that pleased her, because she was also a little apprehensive about leaving our Heavenly Father's presence. I learned that she had been permitted to visit me so that I would know that she was anxiously waiting: I had not hearkened to the message in the baby's crying. She told me she loved me, and as she grew dimmer, I knew I loved her too. Then she was gone.

Not only was she gone, but gone too was the contentment I had been feeling minutes before. I was afraid of another pregnancy; none of the others had been easy ones. In fact, I was usually violently sick through the sixth month, my pregnancy being complicated by toxemia and high blood pressure. Could I handle another pregnancy physically, mentally, or emotionally? Could I handle caring for a fifth child? Could we afford it? How

"I want a hug," you say today,
And smiling, I comply.
Much easier, now that you're
*   here*
Than in your pre-earth life.

—Barbara G. Dykstra
Copyright © 1993
(Used by Permission)

would Michael feel about this? Would he believe me?

With questions like these running through my mind, Michael came home from work. Thinking back, I do not remember exactly how I told him what I had experienced, but was relieved by his reaction. He listened quietly, asked several questions about what I had been doing before this happened, and how my day had gone, what I had learned and what the little girl had looked like. I felt some of my fears and apprehension melt away as we talked.

He was excited. I was overwhelmed!

My next prayer was not over the kitchen sink, but I knelt and poured out my heart to God. First of all, I thanked Him for allowing this little spirit to come visit me and for what I had learned. I asked Him to confirm the truth of what I had seen and heard. I poured out my fears and feelings of apprehension of going through another pregnancy and caring for another child. Before closing my prayer, I asked Him to assure me that I would be able to handle all the responsibilities I faced, as well as another pregnancy. Then I listened very carefully for an answer, clearing my mind of all my worries. The sweetest feeling of peace surrounded me, and I felt as if Heavenly Father's arms were around me, giving me the

Will you see the infancy of this sublime and celestial greatness? Those pure and virgin apprehensions I had in my infancy, and that divine light wherewith I was born...I was a little stranger which at my entrance into the world was saluted and surrounded with innumerable joys. My knowledge was divine; I knew by intuition those things which since my apostasy I collected again by the highest reason.

—Thomas Traherne
The Poetical Works of Thomas
Traherne

reassurance I needed: that everything would be all right, that everything would be taken care of, and that I must trust in Him.

Over the next couple of days I felt my daughter's presence very strongly. I felt as if she were following me around the house as I did my chores. I felt that she wanted to be around me!

Both Michael and I felt so strongly about what had happened that we immediately began making preparations for another pregnancy, considering girl names and checking out hospitals and doctors. The next month I was pregnant.

The pregnancy proved to be more difficult than the other four. At times I wondered if we had made the right choice. We decided to try to have this baby with a mid-wife. During the last eight weeks, I was confined to bed because of toxemia and high blood pressure. My biggest fear throughout it all, however, was that this little baby would be a boy and I would have to go through it all again to get the little girl I had seen.

On March 15, 1989, with my boys sleeping at their Grammy's, I delivered the baby at home with the help of my mid-wife and husband. Eight pounds eleven ounces and twenty-one inches of calm, bright-eyed GIRL!

And it came to pass that [Jesus] did teach and minister unto the children of the multitude of whom hath been spoken, and he did loose their tongues, and they did speak unto their fathers great and marvelous things, even greater than he had revealed unto the people; and he loosed their tongues that they could utter.

—3 Nephi 26:14

I am deeply grateful for my experience, and for our daughter, Bethanie Camilla. She is one of the great joys of our lives. The life I thought was so full before, would be empty without this choice little person in our family.

—*Janet M.*

And the spirit shall return unto God who gave it.

—*Solomon*

Called by Another Name

The prompting had come before. It was time for another baby. I had ignored the impressions at first, dismissed them later as we prepared to move to another state, and then blocked them as we settled into a new home, schools, and neighborhood. "Four is enough!" my in-laws had told us.

I had not approached my husband about this, but one day he turned our light conversation to a heavier tone and said, "Honey, I know you have felt uprooted by the move, and challenged by church responsibilities and that you are trying to settle the kids into new schools and friendships and all, but I have felt all summer that it is time for another baby." I knew in my heart he was right. Someone was missing.

Four months passed, and I was not expecting a baby yet. This was a real surprise, for babies had come so easily and quickly to our home.

One morning, I had gotten up early to weed the yard. I felt impressed that *now* was the time to try to conceive this baby. But I had other things to do, and I had decided, "If it happens, it happens—I'm not going out of my way to get pregnant." I continued to dress. Then I stopped.

The prompting came again, but this time a sort of vision accompanied it. In my mind I saw a graduation ceremony of which I was a spectator. As each successive graduate was called, I was drawn to one young man in particular. He was nice in appearance and stood straight and self-assured. I wanted to know him—to know more about him. I thought he might be someone I knew, but when his name was called, it was not familiar.

Then a powerful thought entered my mind. Unless I returned to conceive this child right then, he would be called by that unfamiliar name, and he would not be our son. In the scene I yearned desperately for him to know me, but I was a stranger. I wanted this child.

Nine months later, a son was born to our family. This beautiful, intense little child, that plays and works with such a zeal for living, needed to come at that time.

—Lois P.

A shadow haunts my every move,
I know him from my dream.
Most people think that four's
 enough,
But not for us, it seems.

—Barbara G. Dykstra
Copyright © 1993
(Used by Permission)

This is Your Daughter, Virginia

When I met my husband, Wade, I knew that he would make a great father. I also knew that I could not give him children because I had had my fallopian tubes severed when I was twenty-six. Therefore, although I loved him very much and he loved me, I could not marry him until I at least tried to resolve my problem.

I had heard about a reversal of a tubal. I had gone to several doctors and they all told me they could not help me because my surgical tubal had been done by burning instead of tying. They said my chances were very low that I would find anyone to correct it. I had seen ten doctors and they all told me they could not help me. While visiting my eleventh doctor, he said, "I can't do it, but I know a doctor who specializes in this procedure and if anyone can help you, he can."

I called this doctor. It was very hard to get in to see

All souls which were to enter human bodies existed before the creation of the world in the Garden of Eden.

—*R. H. Charles*
The Apocrypha and Pseude-
pigrapha of the Old Testament

him, as he was booked several years in advance. Luckily, I was able to get in after a few months, and the testing began. They found out my hormone level was good and everything checked out except my eggs could not go down into my fallopian tubes. Fortunately, a small portion of my tubes had not been burnt so there was the possibility of reconstructive surgery.

Soon I was scheduled for my first surgery. It was a very delicate surgery that was to last seven hours. During this experience, I stopped breathing. Instantly, I found myself suspended in the air above my body. I could look down and see everything the doctors and nurses were doing. I saw the heart monitor flat and the nurses stirring about. My doctor moved away from me to allow another doctor to come in. I couldn't understand why everyone appeared to be so worried.

In this place I found myself, there was brilliant white light all around me. As my senses became alert, I heard a beautiful sound—it was the sound of peace. I cannot describe it with mortal words, only that a powerful feeling of peace permeated my very being. I could hear spiritual beings moving around behind me in a very calm and orderly manner. I don't know where it came form, but all of a sudden I was holding an infant. There was a personage behind me and he said to me, "This is your daughter, Virginia."

I looked at her and I was so thrilled. Ever since I was a child I had always wanted a blond-haired, blue-eyed little girl. These were the features of the beautiful baby girl I was holding. My fiance Wade had blond hair and blue eyes.

I looked at her and asked, "Her name is Virginia?"

The personage behind me said, "Yes."

I turned around to thank him and all of a sudden the heart monitor starting going again and I was immediately returned to my body. I knew I had been summoned back. I was really sad, and my arms hurt because I wasn't holding that beautiful baby.

When I awoke my doctor was very concerned and he said, "You weren't supposed to do that."

I told one nurse exactly what I had seen her do while I was dead. She was so startled she dropped the tray she was holding at the time.

I decided to tell my doctor what had happened to me while I was dead.

He said to me, "I don't disbelieve you. I believe in miracles. I'm a doctor and most doctors I know, believe in miracles. But getting back to reality, after that episode

And now, O Father, glorify Thou me with thine own self with the glory which I had with Thee before the world was.

—John 17:5

*Take the word "recognize."
...The word says we "re-know"
the concept, as if we knew it once
upon a time, forgot it, but then
recognized it as an old friend. It
is as if all knowledge and all wisdom were contained in our minds,
and when we learn "something
new" we are actually only discov-
ering something that existed in
our self all along.*

*—M. Scott Peck, M.D.
The Road Less Traveled*

we have to wait a considerable amount of time before we go back into surgery."

After I recovered and went home, I called his nurse and said, "Every night after 7:00 p.m., I'm going to stop eating so I can be prepared for surgery if you have a cancellation. I am very anxious to finish my surgery. Please tell the doctor to call me if he has any openings. I'll be ready."

Exactly a month later, they called me. I had the surgery and it was very successful. Two weeks later they did the tests to see if my tubes were open. They were! I proceeded with my plans to marry Wade. I was now very confident that I could give him a child, especially since I had seen little Virginia.

The doctor planned to start fertility drugs in six months. He told me there was no way any fertilization would occur without the drugs. Within three months, I went back to him and told him, "I'm pregnant."

"There is no way you could be pregnant," he said.

"Well, I am," I answered.

"No, you are not pregnant. It is not physically possible for you to get pregnant without the drugs."

It was too early for them to test for a pregnancy so they told me to come back in two weeks, since I had not yet missed a menstrual cycle. In two weeks I came back. The tests were positive. I knew all along this was my Virginia. We chose Rose for her middle name, after my grandmother.

Virginia was very slow in coming to earth, but she was born healthy, strong and beautiful—a mirror-image of the blond-haired, blue-eyed infant I had held when my spirit had left my body during the surgery. The greatest miracle in our lives and our greatest joy is our daughter, Virginia Rose.

—JoAnn B.

From God above Being sent,
The Heavens me enflame...
O how divine Am I!

—Thomas Traherne,
"The Rapture"

Shared Dreams
of an Unborn Child

Coming from a family of eleven children and being the oldest, I have always felt a motherly instinct for my younger siblings. Seeing my mother pregnant has always stirred my soul and awakened my awareness to the importance of motherhood.

One night, I had a dream. My whole family was together. My mother was there with a new-born boy, and I was holding a new-born daughter of my own. I was showing off her beautiful, dark brown eyebrows like those of her mother, and her gorgeous blue gray eyes like those of her father. Time went by, and we had to go, so I put her in the car seat of our truck. As I got into it, my precious child gave me the most beautiful smile I had ever seen. The love she gave was more love than I had ever felt before. Though I am not a mother yet, I felt the love that only a child could give to her mother. I awoke

Unborn

That he and she
Could have been we
Is nothing unusual
In a world full of fields
That could have been flowers

Unborn beauty runs
As far as the eye can see.
And there is he
And there is she.

Occasionally
They almost sense
The almost scent
Of the almost blossom
And have to
Catch their breath.

—*Carol Lynn Pearson*
(Women I have Known & Been,
Aspen Books, 1992, Salt Lake
City, Utah, p. 94)

feeling such tremendous love and a sense of a spirit from my unborn child.

Two months passed, and I was still unable to forget the child I dreamt of that night. As I prayed about this, I came to believe that God gave me a glimpse, a premonition if I may call it that, of the child that I may one day bring into this world. Until that day I will cling to the memory of that loving child I dreamt of that night.

My fiance also dreamt of what might have been the same loving child. It had almost been a week since I initially had my dream when he told me of the dream he had one night. In his dream, he entered a room where my mother and I were standing with a young girl. She lit up and reached out with beautiful, loving eyes and hands. He picked her up and the hug he got was more than words could ever describe. He could see and feel the love in her that together we had formed.

From our dreams we were assured of the precious gift of life. Whether that child is ever born or not, we are both aware of the importance and love that the life of a child can bring. We both now look forward to all of God's wonderful blessings.

—*A young wife*

Not Too Much to Ask

"Mommy."

I raised my head, listening intently. Of course, my sleepy mind realized, one of my daughters needed something.

"Mommy. It's time."

Time for what?

"Mommy," the voice called. "Mommy."

Now awake, but barely so, I threw back the covers and swung my feet over the edge of the bed, peering into the darkness to identify the daughter who needed me.

It must be Christina; Trinell or Melissa would have left the bedroom door open. What I saw, however, was not one of my girls, but a male Indian child. He was clothed in white robes, his arms outstretched.

"Mommy, it's time. It's time for me to come."

I rubbed my eyes, knowing I could not have seen

what I had just seen. My ears must be involved in the trick, too, I reasoned as I snuggled back into my warm bed.

But sleep was not to come. As determined as I was to convince myself the incident had been a dream, someone else was just as determined that I realize it was real. A short time later, I was looking at the same Indian child, clothed as before.

"Mommy, it's time for me to come. Soon I will be coming into the world, and I'm to be your son."

I spent the rest of the night debating whether or not to tell Ray, my husband. Eventually I did, and his reaction was not surprising. He took both my hands in his and told me he would have to also receive personal inspiration on the matter.

I understood and waited patiently. A few months later I was not surprised when my husband related his experience with our son-to-be. While working, he had been listening to some music. Suddenly the music ceased. Peaceful, heavenly strains filled the air and a voice impressed upon Ray's mind and soul that an Indian son was to come into our family. Now was the time for him to start preparations to receive the child.

Our first step was to submit an adoption application

to a social services agency. However, because we already had three children, our application was denied.

Our hearts sank, but we clung to this hope. We believed that we would not have to wait that long.

Two weeks later, we were notified that our application was being reviewed. A short time later, we were notified that our application had been accepted. But again, we were warned of the three to five-year wait.

At this time I needed reassurance. And comfort did come through a beautiful prayer experience. I was reassured that our son would soon be with us and he was to be called Mathew.

On 27 July 1984, a boy was born in Canada. Carefully, a nurse washed and bundled him in blankets. Then, placing him in a hospital bassinet, she wheeled him to a private nursery. He was being placed for adoption.

A few doors down the hall, a young mother was sealing an envelope. She had the grace and bearing acquired from her Blackfoot heritage. She knew in her heart that what she was doing was right. She handed the envelope to a social worker.

Inside the envelope was her story. She told briefly of her own history and her desire to provide her child

If we all realized that we were the children of one father, we would stop shouting at each other as much as we do.

—George Bernard Shaw

SATURDAY'S WARRIOR

*Who are these children coming
    down
Coming down like gentle rain thru
    darkened skies.
With glory trailing from their feet
    as they go
And endless promise in their
    eyes?
Who are these young ones grow-
    ing tall
Like silver trees against the
    storm?
Who will not bend with the wind
    or the change
But stand to fight the world alone.*

*Strangers from a realm of light
Who have forgotten all
The memory of their former life
The purpose of their call
And so they must learn why
    they're here
And who they really are
They must learn why they're here
    and who they are.*

*—Doug Stewart
Embryo Music
(Used by Permission)*

with the best possible life. She had prayed that her child would be blessed with a good home. And if it was not too much to ask, she had added, she would like the family to have girls.

It was not too much to ask. In the late summer of 1984, we received a call asking us to come to Calgary to pick up our son. As they placed him in my arms and his tiny hand curled around Ray's finger, we knew at last that Mathew was home.

—Cheryl C.[6]

A Pre-Existent Expression of Love

I had reached those last few weeks of pregnancy. As I tried to sleep, I noted in my mind, that it was a sacrifice to be willing to endure a degree of discomfort to bring forth life. I was happy and willing to do so, but I was just making note that these last few weeks are the most difficult. With three pillows for support, I finally found a position in which I felt I could fall asleep.

A feeling of contentment and peace settled over me and I became aware of someone standing near my bed. I saw a fully grown spirit dressed in a gleaming white garment, falling in loose pleats from the waist and loosely fitted above. His countenance shone and he spoke to me. He thanked me for my willingness to provide an earthly tabernacle for him, and he expressed his love. Then he was gone. Three weeks later I gave birth to my eleventh son. He has been a very loving child, ever full of spontaneous hugs and "thank you's."

—Carol E.[7]

*For I know them and before
they came into being I took
knowledge of them, and on their
faces I set my seal.*

—Odes of Solomon 8:16, 21

"I Have Your Name on Me"

We had tried for ten years to have children but were not successful. We became discouraged as the realization settled heavily on us that we would probably never have children. After discussing this with some good friends, they suggested we consider adoption.

One night shortly after this, I was having a nightmare. Suddenly in my dream there was a light and a peaceful feeling. In the light I saw a beautiful baby with big dark eyes. Peace came over me. He said, "I have been waiting a long time and I have your name on me." He spoke these words as one adult speaks to another, but I saw a baby's face. I did not know if the baby was a boy or girl.

Shortly, we made plans to adopt a child. It seemed to be the right thing to do, and we were excited. Within

The First Race
Traditions by the Osage Elders

The First of the race
Was saying, "Ho, younger broth-
er! the children
have no bodies.
"We shall seek bodies for our
children.
"Ho, younger brother! you shall
attend to it."
They reached one upper world
and stood.
There they were not human
beings.
"Ho, younger brother! the chil-
dren have no bodies
he was saying.
"We must seek bodies for our
children."

(Smithsonian Institution—Bureau
of Ethnology, Sixth Annual
Report 1884-85, Osage
Traditions, Rev. J. Owen
Dorsey, 1888, p. 388. Quoted
in The Gospel of the Great
Spirit, by Joshua Moses
Bennett, Morningstar
Publishing Company, Inc.,
1990, p. 197.
Used by Permission.)

the year, we finally received our phone call. The baby we were to adopt was born!

We had to wait 72 hours before we could pick up our son, Todd. Two days after his birth, we were told the birth mother wanted to see him. This was not a good sign. In about 90% of those cases the mother keeps the baby. I sat in my office praying. Suddenly I felt the presence of my step father, who had passed away many years previous. He assured me that all was well. I realized that it was the anniversary of my step father's death.

The adoption went fine—without complications. We were grateful to at last have our little child.

Three years later my sister had an experience in which my step father (her father), appeared to her in a dream. He told her: "Todd is a great spirit and was my good friend in the Spirit World. When he found out his birth parents didn't want to keep him, I asked him if he would come to our family. Todd agreed."

—Jerry and Dorothy

A Letter to My Son

The following is an edited letter from a mother to her son whom she put up for adoption. She wrote it shortly after his birth and handed it to the adoptive parents to give him when he came of age to understand.

My precious son,

I do not know how you feel toward me and the decision I made about your adoption, but I trust your parents, and they must feel you are ready to know the circumstances of how you came to be.

At the time I became pregnant with you, the relationship with my parents was suffering severely because of my negative attitude. I had just turned seventeen.

Eventually, with the greatly needed help of a church leader, I told my parents of the pregnancy, and we proceeded with making plans on what to do. After much counsel and prayer, and after weighing all possibilities, I made the decision to have you and give you up for adoption. Our parents agreed that your father was yet too young to marry.

My parents felt I should live with a foster family in another state until after the birth, and arrangements were made. I now understand the wisdom of their decision, but at the time, I was angry and felt as if I was being "put away" to hide their shame. I did not want to go, and as the time for me to leave drew near, I became desperate to find a way to stay at home.

I had always been strongly opposed to abortion, but with these difficult pressures, I found myself thinking about it occasionally, and even considering it. If I could just remove the presence of the baby, I could go on with my life and everything could go on as it had been. No more problem. No fears. No shame. No facing up to my mistake.

The idea of having an abortion actually started to sound like my solution. I really did not *want* an abortion, but I was feeling desperate! I knew I had to act quickly as my flight was scheduled to leave within a few days. Each clinic I called was unable to fit me into their sched-

I want to tell you, each and every one of you, that you are well acquainted with God our heavenly Father, or the great Eloheim. You are all well acquainted with Him, for there is not a soul of you but what has lived in His house and dwelt with Him year after year; and yet you are seeking to become acquainted with Him, when the fact is, you have merely forgotten what you did know.

— Brigham Young

ule until well after my flight out of state.

I was emotionally exhausted when I finally hung up the phone. I went into my room, turned off the light, and crawled into bed where I cried myself to sleep. It has been many years since that night, but I can still remember the dream I had as clearly as if it were yesterday.

In my dream, it was a few weeks before your scheduled delivery date, and I was lying on a table in the doctor's office having an examination. The doctor wanted to make sure that you were growing properly and wanted to take your weight and measurements. He made an incision in my abdomen and carefully removed you from my womb. I watched as he had you weighed and measured. Everything was just fine and you were developing normally into a fine, healthy baby. I was enjoying the experience, yet at the same time I was still searching for a way in which I should not have to follow through with the whole ordeal. For a moment, I considered telling the doctor not to put you back into my womb: to stitch me up and just let me walk away.

Furthermore we have had fathers of our flesh which corrected us, and we gave them reverence: shall we not much rather be in subjection unto the Father of spirits, and live?

—Hebrews 12:8

But at that moment a wonderful thing happened. You suddenly turned your head and reached out for me, your big eyes glistening with tears. I could not resist the urge to pick you up. As I held you close, you wrapped your tiny arms around my neck with the strength of an adult and would not let me put you down. I could feel your desperation to cling to life, and I knew then that it was a small sacrifice for me to provide that life for you. The doctor and his office slowly faded away, and you and I were left alone, still clinging to each other.

When I awoke the next morning, I told my mother about the dream. I told her that now I knew without a doubt that my child had a right to live: a right to be born into this world and experience the joys, as well as the sorrows, that this life can bring. My sweet son, please believe me when I say how much I love you!

I thought over every possible solution concerning my keeping and raising you myself, but there were just too many factors mounted against it. I prayed to keep you but I never felt good about it. I know I made the right decision in having you adopted, but it is the hardest thing I have ever done. You were such a beautiful baby, and I loved you so much.

I felt that another couple that was prepared to start a family, but could have none of their own, would be able to provide for you far more adequately than I. With me, your life would start in shame, guilt, sorrow, and without a father to love you as your adoptive father now loves

The universe resounds with the joyful cry I am.

—*Scriabin*

you.

I truly believe that we are, in some way, assigned children in our pre-earth existence. At one point as I deliberated, I wondered if I might be giving up one of my assigned children by placing you up for adoption. But before I reached a conclusion, I had another thought. What happens to the children assigned to a couple who are physically unable to have any of their own? The moment I had that question, it was answered in my mind. The couples adopt them. Each time the child seems to fit so perfectly into the family. I then realized that I was actually carrying a child that had been assigned to another couple. I hope you understand. Even though I am the person who carried you and gave you birth, your mom and dad are actually your true parents!

Though all my wishes are that I could watch you grow up to be a handsome young man, I know deep in my heart that I have done the right thing. I hope someday in the eternities, we may meet and share our feelings face to face. I love you son, and always, always will.

Forever my love,
Mom

We rejoice in the thrill of fatherhood. To be co-creators with our beloved wives is an honor that goes beyond all other honors and a responsibility that dwarfs all other responsibilities. Being trusted by our Heavenly Father to receive one of his own spirit children is a most divine opportunity and to prepare that child to someday return to his or her heavenly home is a responsibility beyond description.

—George Durrant

The Veil of Forgetfulness Was Not Yet Complete

For Christmas, I was assembling Books of Remembrance for each of my eleven children. Each book was to contain a picture history of the child from birth to his present age along with pictures of his parents, grandparents, etc. I had pictures scattered all over our large kitchen table.

Jason had climbed right up in the middle of them when I tried to lift him down. "Gama!" he said, pointing to a picture of a young woman. "Gama!" he said again. I took him in my arms and showed him the picture again.

"Do you mean Grandma Hazel?" I asked.

"No!" he insisted. "Gama!"

My mother is living and he calls her "Gama Hazo." The young woman in the picture was his paternal grandmother, Vivian, who had died four years before Jason was born. His living grandmother was much older than the grandmother I thought he had never seen, and the picture was taken at a much younger age. There was no mistake—they did not look alike. This incident indicated to us that his veil of forgetfulness was not complete from a former, heavenly existence.

—Carol E.[8]

O God, the God of the spirits of all flesh, shall one man sin, and wilt Thou be wroth with all the congregation?

—Numbers 16:22

Difficult Delivery

I was in the midst of a difficult delivery. All seemed dark and the tears coursed down my cheeks. I had endured natural childbirth six times before, but given the choice of death to release me from delivery at that moment, I may have chosen it. My husband, John, leaned forward and whispered, "Courage, for your little one will come very soon."

Then, at the most bleak moment, I saw my deceased mother, holding a small boy by the hand. Just as suddenly, she was gone. Our baby boy, Ben was born half an hour later.

—*Lois P.*
Mesa, Arizona

The Spirits I Felt Were My Granddaughters

One Summer, I began to feel that perhaps I was to have more children. I had nine children and was 48 years old. As I prayed and pondered the next several months, I felt that two more girls were going to be a part of my family. I fasted several times and continued to ask about them.

One day as I was feeling especially depressed and worried, I felt these two girls embrace me and reassure me that all would be well. As the tears flowed, I felt their love and concern.

In the next two years, two of my daughters-in-law gave birth to girls. After the second was born, I felt impressed that these were the girls I was expecting to

DAY-OLD CHILD

My day-old child lay in my arms
    with my lips against his ear.
I whispered strong, "How I
    wish—I wish that you could
    hear.

"I've a hundred wonderful things
    to say
(a tiny cough and a nod),
Hurry, hurry, hurry and grow
So I can tell you about God."

My day-old baby's mouth was
    still and my words only tickled
    his ear.
But a kind of a light passed
    through his eyes, and I saw
    this thought appear:

"How I wish I had a voice and
    words; I've a hundred things to
    say.
Before I forget I'd tell you of
    God—
I left Him yesterday."

        —Carol Lynn Pearson,
Beginnings, (Bookcraft, SLC: UT
                    1979, p. 42)

become a part of my family. As I have held and cared for them, I feel that they are as surely "my children" as any I have given birth to.

—Ann H.

"No, Mama. Please Don't"

When I was sixteen I had a cyst that hemorrhaged inside my ovary. The attending doctor explained that there had been a great deal of damage to the ovary. He also told me that my womb was tipped, and I was only ovulating once a year. Taking all these factors into consideration, he concluded that I had a very slim chance of conceiving a child.

This problem did not really concern me as my aspirations at that time were to get my driver's license and pass finals. Then, over time—and especially as I became engaged—I began to dream of marriage and starting a family.

After I told my fiance what the doctor had said, we prepared ourselves for the possibility of adoption. Much of the counsel we received from others was to postpone trying to have children until our college educations were finished. Then with a secure job situation, we could start

Before my Tongue or Cheeks were
*   to me shewn,*
Before I knew my Hands were
*   mine,*
Or that my Sinews did my
*   Members joyn,*
When neither Nostril, Foot, or
*   Ear,*
As yet was seen or felt, or did
*   appear;*
I was within
A House I knew not, newly
*   clothed with Skin.*

Then was my Soul my only All to
*   me.*
A Living Endless Eye,
Just bounded with the Skie
Whose Power, whose Act, whose
*   Essence was to see.*
I was an inward Sphere of Light,
Or an Interminable Orb of Sight,
An Endless and a Living Day,
A vital Sun that round about did
*   ray*
All Life, all Sence,
A Naked Simple Pure Intelligence.

—Thomas Traherne
"The Preparative"
The Poetical Works of Thomas
Traherne

our family. This caused a conflict within me because of my fear of missing those few times I would be most able to conceive.

After much prayer, we determined our chances of having a family would be better if we did not use birth control. Having children had become our priority and we felt good about this decision for a couple of months.

As our wedding date grew nearer, temporal logic won over heavenly inspiration and we bought some contraceptives. We were married on a Friday night. By the following Tuesday morning, during our honeymoon, I had begun to feel very anxious. I explained my feelings to my husband, and he suggested we fast and pray about it once more. That night I had a dream.

In the dream, I found myself completely surrounded by darkness. Suddenly, a doorway appeared with an intense, bright light shining from it. I raised my right hand to shield my eyes from the brightness. After a moment I was able to focus. I saw what I presumed to be three young children. The light from behind them created a shadow so I could only see the outline of their forms. All three appeared to be boys. I remember making note of the shape of their heads and the way the tips of their ears stuck out. The one in the middle was the tallest and he held the hands of the other two.

Next, I noticed I was holding something in my left hand. I raised it up to get a closer look and recognized the contraceptives we had been using. At almost the same instant the child in the middle pleaded with me, "No mama, please don't!" I never saw his face, but I knew it was he who had said it.

Instantly, I found myself awake in our hotel room. I woke my husband, and told him my experience. We decided not to use contraceptives, and nine months later our first son was born.

He was followed by two more boys. Each one has cute little ears that stick out a bit. We now have five children. The oldest has a fetish about holding the hands of his younger siblings which sort of aggravates them. I tell them he cannot help it, he has always done it!

I am so grateful to our first child who had such a great desire to come to our family. Through contact with him we were able to put self-gratification and pursuit of worldly accomplishment in proper perspective. We accepted our responsibility—and joy, I might add—to have children. I know this stewardship was accepted in a "life" before this life.

—*Caleb and Nyla L.*

For all souls are prepared to eternity, before the formation of the world.

—*Second Enoch*

My Own Baby

"Mommy; when I grow up, will I have my own babies?"

"Sure you will Sweetheart. You are a sweet, obedient girl, and you are wonderful with children. Don't you even worry: you will be a wonderful mommy someday."

At age fourteen, I still asked, "Mom; when I grow up, will I have MY OWN babies?"

Of course, she still answered, "Sure you will, sweetheart."

I still wanted to believe this was true, but I could not. I wanted children of my own: conceiving and bearing each precious child. But I sensed a vague, mysterious feeling that raised suspicion and caused uneasiness within me. I tried to ignore and suppress it, but this unwanted feeling persisted, as if to threaten my cherished dreams and goals.

"Doctor, will I be able to have babies of MY

OWN?" My husband, Kevin, and I were now nearly three years into our childless marriage. I was hoping to hear the same comforting answer from my doctor that I had received from my mother for so many years. I could tell by his expression that this would not be the case. With a few strokes of his pen, I embarked on a wrenching journey: six-and-a half years of infertility testing, pelvic exams, ultra sounds, fertility drugs, surgeries, fasts, blessings, marital and financial stress, hopes, disappointments, frustrations.

I came from the house of my Father in a far land, and I shall mount up until I return to that land of the pure.

—The Psalm of Thomas
Old Testament and Related
Studies
(Hugh Nibley)

One night, during a particular period of my life filled with self pity, hot-flashes and painful ovarian cysts, I had a sweet dream. It lasted only a matter of seconds, yet was so impressive and distinct that I shall never forget it. The back-ground was completely black. Suddenly, a beautiful baby girl, about eight months old, appeared. She looked just like a China doll: fresh, creamy, white skin with rosy cheeks; blonde hair fashioned into a "whale-spout" pony tail; and penetrating blue eyes. She was positioned as if posing for a photograph. She wore a soft, frilly red and white dress. Most impressive of all were her beautiful smile and dimple in her left cheek. Her presence radiated a feeling of goodness, bringing a sweet, genuinely happy feeling over me. She disappeared as quickly as she had appeared, and the dream ended.

I awoke and lay in bed for hours savoring that happy feeling, waiting to share my dream with Kevin when he awoke. "She looked kind of like your sister's new baby," I told him, trying to rationalize the significance of my dream.

A year or so later, I had a second dream. It began as my first dream—with total blackness. A baby girl appeared out of nowhere again. This baby was about eighteen months old, wearing pink corduroy overalls and a pink jacket. She toddled toward me, arms outstretched, reaching upward, as if bodily asking to be picked up. I saw that she was the same baby from my other dream, complete with creamy skin, rosy cheeks, penetrating blue eyes, whale-spout pony tail, beautiful smile and dimpled left cheek. I reached down to pick her up. As my hands neared her body to lift her, she disappeared and I brought back empty arms. I awoke immediately, wondering what it all meant.

Time passed, as did more physical and emotional pain, more medical testing, and my final surgery. My doctors had finally determined the cause of my infertility, and had recommended adoption for us. I was heart-broken. Why was this happening to me? I had done every-

It is better that the mother discover her child by touching it. Better to feel before she sees. Better to sense this warm and trembling life, to be moved in her heart by what her hands tell her. To hold her child rather than merely look at it.

—Frederick Leboyer,
Birth Without Violence

*Your faith in me must be complete
divine—more trusting than I know
as unearthly, unearthed, you wait
for invitation to our home.*

*Knowing in that forgotten world
How I would wish for rest this
    time,
would want your brother, fifth
    child, the last,
You took your place, sixth, sure,
    in line.*

*The children have forgotten now
the color of your hair and eyes
but they, like me, at moments still
notice spaces, wondering why.*

*And now, your brother still a baby
not yet sitting on his own
I feel your eyes close on my days
not anxious but unmoored, alone.*

*You wait, with faith still perfect—
    white
for welcome to our hectic home
and I—I'm overpowered, trem-
    bling
at what we've always, always
    known.*

—C. Emily Ellsworth
© 1989

thing I knew to prepare to be an outstanding mother. I had read child-rearing books, taken child psychology classes, baby-sat practically the entire town, exercised, ate right. I had even majored in early childhood education in college. Now my hopes and dreams were shattered. I felt like an outcast.

It took two long, painful years for me to heal emotionally, and spiritually and accept the idea of adopting someone else's child. Our adoption case worker told us that the waiting period for a baby would be anywhere from two to four years. We were not getting any younger, and I wanted children now, not in four years! I wondered how much more anxiety and disappointment I was going to have to endure.

Teaching school seemed to be my life-saver. My sweet little first-graders partially filled my void, as did the young children's class I taught in church.

One night, shortly after we had moved into a new home, I had yet a third dream. This dream lasted for a long time, yet even now I can vividly recall the whole thing. In it, an adoption agent came to the door with a child. My husband was away, so I went to the neighbor's to show off my gift. While I should have been elated after such a long wait, I could feel nothing but a knot: as if something was terribly wrong. This baby was not for us. He would not let me love him, and nothing I did would soothe him. Yet how could I tell the agent? What would our chances be of getting another child if we were to turn down this one?

The next day (in the dream), I called the case worker to come take the baby; he belonged to someone else. As we stood talking—a jungle of emotions in my heart—the case worker said, "Just a minute." He went out to his car and returned with another baby: a smaller baby wrapped in a fuzzy pink bunting. "How would you like this baby?" he asked, with excitement in his voice and a sparkle in his eye. Exhilaration rushed my body and soul as I looked down at her face.

Yes! Yes! this was my baby. Our eyes met, our souls touched. It was her: the little blonde-haired, blue-eyed, dimple-cheeked China doll! I knew it with every fiber of my being! I engulfed this precious, beautiful angel and whirled around and around with her. No earthly words could describe my exhilaration, my joy, my jubilation!

Then I heard a buzzing sound. As I fumbled to turn off my alarm clock, I realized I had only been dreaming. It seemed so real, though! Could these wonderful dreams

The Lord designed and devised me, and He prepared me before the foundation of the world, that I should be the mediator of His Covenant.

—The Assumption of Moses

be a sign from heaven? I hoped so. Oh, I hoped so.

About two and a half weeks later, I awoke with pain in my abdomen. "Oh no," I thought, "not another tumor!" Throughout the day, the pain grew steadily stronger. The next day the pain was severe, and increased even more the day after that, prompting me to finally give in and call the doctor. The nurse on the phone made an appointment for two days away. I hoped I would not die by then. Her diagnosis of severe gall bladder (stones) attacks did not seem to fit my symptoms: severe abdominal pain; nausea, but no fever or chills; a sensation of warmth in my abdomen; restlessness; fatigue.

That evening, we received a phone call from our adoption agent. "We have a baby for you and... Blah, blah, blah," was all I heard after that.

A BABY! For a fleeting moment, the thrill and shock of it all overtook me. What sex? How old? Healthy? So much to find out.

Yes, it was a girl, six pounds, four ounces, twenty and one-half inches long. Yes, keep going... Dark hair.

Stop! My baby has blonde hair! I wanted a baby, but the right baby. Could my dreams really have meant something? Could they have mislead me? Could I take

Everything in our life happens as though we entered upon it with a load of obligations contracted in a previous existence...obligations whose sanction is not of this present life, [which] seems to belong to a different world, founded on kindness, scruples, sacrifice, a world entirely different from this one, a world whence we emerge to be born on this earth, before returning thither.

—Marcel Proust, in Gabriel Marcel, Homo Viator (New York: Harper and Row, 1963) p. 8.

and love this baby anyway? Could her dark hair turn blonde as she got older?

Kevin and I hung up the phone and prayed about whether we were to accept this little girl into our home. We both felt good about it, and decided that we did indeed want this baby. I was happy, fearful, anxious, and so tired—but much too excited to sleep this night.

The next day, we drove to the agency to receive our child. After what felt like years, a door opened, and in walked a young lady carrying a tiny pink bundle. My heart pounded wildly. A myriad of emotions rushed at me: excitement, curiosity, nervousness, reverence, fear, hope—hope that this really was the baby of my dreams. I took her gently in my arms and surveyed my beautiful treasure. She did not look like the China doll in my dreams, but somehow she did fit into our family. Amazingly, she looked a lot like Kevin with his coloring and features.

We stroked her fresh, baby-soft skin; smelled her fragrant newborn scent; kissed her tiny fingers. We giggled gleefully, like excited children at Christmas. We lovingly embraced and wept tears of joy together. Our surroundings no longer existed to us. We were totally immersed in our own new world of wonderment and awe

I
Did not plant you,
True
But when
The season is done—
When the alternate
Prayers for sun
And for rain
Are counted—
When the pain
Of weeding
And the pride
Of watching
Are through—
Then
I will hold you
High
A shining sheaf
Above the thousand
Seeds grown wild.

Not my planting,
But by heaven
My harvest—
My own child.

—Carol Lynn Pearson
Beginnings
(Book Craft, Salt Lake City,
Utah, 1985)

LOOK AT THE BABY

Look at the baby, oh, look at her
*   eyes.*
What do you think she can see?
For she smiles rather strangely
And stares at the skies;
I know she's not looking at me.

Do you think she is smiling at
*   angels*
Hovering ever so near?
Maybe they're telling her secrets
You and I can't hear.

Look at the baby, oh, look at her
*   smile.*
What is she trying to say?
Do you think she gets lonely each
*   once in a while*
So angels came calling today?

For the angels and baby were
*   play-mates*
In heaven before she was born
And maybe they're lonely for their
*   little friend*
On this beautiful sun-shiny morn.

© *Janeen Brady,*
Brite Music Enterprises
Salt Lake City, Utah, 84109
(Used with Permission)

with this child. She was precious and perfect.

"Hi Baby. Do you know who we are? We're your Mommy and Daddy." It was hard to believe I was actually saying that! She opened her eyes and gazed at us, as if to acknowledge that she knew who we were. There was definitely something special about this baby!

Though we were not permitted to meet Jessica's birth mother, we learned the history and some of her autobiographical information. What we learned pleased us and created within us a deep sense of gratitude and admiration for her. I asked about the birth mother's labor and delivery, and learned that she had gone into labor Monday morning and delivered Tuesday. She had a fairly painful labor and after-birth pains until Wednesday evening. "How do you like that?" I remarked. Her birth mother and I were in pain at the same time for the same length of time." Apparently, many adoptive parents experience vicarious labor with their birth mothers.

"Can you tell us any more about the birth parents?" we asked. We were amazed at the incredible similarities between them and Kevin and I. God's wisdom seemed evident in bringing us together.

"She is so alert! She looks just like the two of you. You would never know she was adopted! She is adorable!" These were the comments we so gleefully received as the days went on. I was loving being a mommy. Little Amy Jessica was everything any parent could ever wish for—or dream for.

One day, as Christmas time neared, I lovingly bathed and dressed little Amy Jessica in her frilly red and white velvet Christmas dress. As I put the bow in her hair and stood back for a final overview, I suddenly saw that blonde haired, dimpled cheeked, blue eyed China doll. The baby in my dreams was sitting right there in front of me, posed just as I had seen her in my first dream so many years ago! She was radiant.

I stared at her in humble awe. Faith ran through my soul. No longer did I feel an outcast. I knew Heavenly Father loved me. This precious little child, though born of another woman, was given to me. She was truly MY OWN baby.

Gird up now thy loins like a man; for I will demand of thee, and answer thou me. Where wast thou when I laid the foundations of the earth? When the morning stars sang together, and all the sons of God shouted for joy?

—Job 38: 3, 4, 7

—*Melinda Price*
Lawrence, Kansas

Companion Child

Every time I went to the physician during the early months of my handicapped daughter's life, the attending doctor and nurse would encourage me to prohibit the conception of future children. They emphasized that I did not know how much care this child would require through the years, and they reminded me of the possibility of other children having the same disability.

This contradicted a blessing I had received by the laying on of hands by a beloved church leader. In this blessing, he indicated that the Lord had promised me sons and daughters reserved for my home. So far I had two daughters and one son. I wanted to have all the children the Lord intended me to have.

One evening just prior to falling asleep, for just an instant, I beheld a baby. This snap-shot vision revealed a baby sitting upright, smiling, and appearing very robust and healthy. Our daughter, who was handicapped, was quite thin by comparison. I was filled with the Holy Ghost as I prayed about this little spirit being ours and if it were time to proceed with this pregnancy.

Our third little daughter was born nine months and two days following this special preview. She was indeed born healthy and was such a joy from day one. Our handicapped daughter seemed to rally with her birth. Having this little one seemed to accelerate, not impede, her progress. I will be ever grateful for His input and guidance on this all-important decision.

—*Vicki R.*[9]

Before I formed thee in the belly I knew thee: and before thou camest forth out of the womb I sanctified thee....

—*Jeremiah 1:5*

Who Are You?

Clearing away the morning dishes on a beautiful warm and sunny Spring day, I was feeling an amazing contentment with my life. My husband and I had a new home, a beautiful family, and a wonderful marriage. It seemed that we had everything that anyone could want or need.

When the doorbell rang and interrupted my thoughts, I assumed that it was my neighbor. She had phoned earlier in the day about a lost dog and mentioned that she would soon be over. But when I opened the door, there stood a strange man. Before I realized what I had done, I had allowed him into my home. He said he needed to use my phone because of car troubles. I knew immediately that I had placed myself in great danger. Before I had time to think, he was pointing a gun at me. I was in a daze as he proceeded to assault me.

A babe in a house is a well-spring of pleasure.

—*Martin Farquhar Tupper*
from "Of Education"

After locking me in my bathroom, the stranger ransacked my house. I had a feeling of calm come over me and I asked the Lord: "Please, if this man is going to kill me, let it be swift. Please take care of my family, and please carry their grief." My fear began to totally vanish as I felt a presence beside me. Although I saw no one, the presence was unmistakable that of a young woman: gentle and kind. I said out loud, "Who are you?"

I sensed that this spirit essence was a blood relative and I assumed that this was a guardian angel that was going to take me to the other side should I be killed. The presence was so powerful that I knew this person was in charge of the situation now; not the criminal. My mind was not on the criminal; although he was still in my home. My mind was on this unseen person who was with me. Finally I heard the intruder leave, and almost immediately thereafter I felt my spiritual friend depart.

I managed to unlock the bathroom door then run outside my house. As the sun warmed my face, I felt so thankful to be alive! I thought, "Thank you God for letting me live. I will be okay."

I never spoke to anyone about my experience with the unseen comforter—partly because it was very personal in nature. The focus now was on the crime and the opportunity did not arise to talk about it.

Ten months later, after six and a half years of wanting another child, I was delighted to find myself pregnant. I knew I was having a girl. I told the doctor, my friends, and relatives. There was no doubt in my mind, although many of them teased me for my confidence.

On the night my baby was born, as I was watching this great miracle take place, it was almost like there was an aura around her head. All attending were in awe at the beauty of this great occasion.

When the doctor had cleaned her off somewhat and made sure that she was breathing well, he placed her in my arms. It was as though everyone else in the room faded into the background, and she and I were alone. I looked into her eyes and her focus caught mine. Her little eyes became transfixed on me and we had an immediate bond. I said, "It was you." No one else knew what I meant, but I knew she did.

It was very strange to have this precious little life— so new—and yet for me to have the knowledge of the strength and power of her spirit. It was as though she had been watching me for a long time. I felt that this child had been my protector before her birth.

The Lord bore witness to me that this day was the

A little child born yesterday, A thing on mother's milk and kisses fed.

—Homer
from "Hymn to Hermes"

reason my life was spared: so that I could bring her to earth. No matter what other honors may come to me in this life, my greatest accomplishment will be that of being granted the opportunity of being a mother.

—Name withheld by request

My Little Girl and My Friend Lee

In 1963 all of us in my high school graduation class felt helplessly caught up in the turmoil of Vietnam and other agitations of the times. Each of us wondered how the current events would affect us.

After one year at the University of Utah and two years off for a mission for the LDS Church in Scotland, I re-enrolled at the University taking ROTC and Men's Chorus, among other classes.

I met Lee in Men's Chorus where he was the President. Having just returned from a mission in England, Lee and I were the same ages. We often double-dated during the school year with Marilyn and her friend Julie. When Marilyn and I were engaged, I told Lee he ought to be thinking seriously about Julie. They always had a lot of fun together and seemed to be a perfect match. Though he liked her a lot, Lee was hesitant to get too involved.

During Spring Quarter of 1967, Lee and I both received notices that unless we raised our grade point averages we would not be able to retain our student deferments from the draft. We both studied very hard. By the end of the quarter my grades were high enough but Lee's were not.

On June 19, 1967, Marilyn and I were married. Lee attended our reception and Julie manned our guest book.

Lee was drafted and ordered to active duty on August 5, 1967. Lee was such an outstanding soldier that after basic and advance individual training, he took the battery of tests and applied for Officer's Candidate School. He was accepted and graduated and then went on to Ranger School in May, 1969 where he was named Officer Honor Graduate.

I continued on at the University. For nearly three years Marilyn and I had been trying to start our family. We had even been approved for adopting a baby, but eventually turned down the opportunity. Sometime in October, 1969 my wife announced that she was pregnant and was due the first of June, 1970. What joyous news. We were both so excited and anxious to share our news

There's only one pretty child in the world, and every mother has it.

—Chesire Proverb

with all our friends.

Lee came home on leave, December 1969. I was teaching Release Time Seminary for the LDS Church at Kearns Jr. High School in Salt Lake City Utah, and was taking a couple of correspondence courses in order to graduate. I had Lee spend the day with me at the Seminary and talk to each of my classes. He told them about his training and what it meant to him to be a member of the Church of Jesus Christ of Latter-day Saints and to be an officer in the U.S. Army. He spoke with conviction and power. Both I and the students were touched.

Lee came over to our apartment after Christmas, just before he was to leave for Vietnam. We ate, joked, talked and reminisced. When my wife got up and left the room for a minute, Lee turned to me. "Roy," he said, "I've come to say good-bye. I have to go now. I want to thank you for your friendship. I'm going on another mission, only I'm not coming back from this one."

I looked at him intently, trying to understand his meaning and then I threw my arms around him, hugged him, and thanked him for his friendship. "Lee, you take care of yourself," I said, "because I won't be far behind you." I was scheduled to get commissioned as a 2nd Lieutenant on 23 March 1970, and I knew I would be

We experience "sudden surges of deja vu" wherein intuition and intimations from beyond the veil remind us of who we were and who we may become.

—Neal A. Maxwell,
Speaches of the Year, 1978,
p. 152

trained and over in Vietnam within the year.

On April 30, 1970, President Richard Nixon announced that U.S. troops had begun a ground offensive against Communist bases in Cambodia; the U.S. 1st Cavalry Division and the ARVN Airborne Division, totalling more than 40,000 troops, launched the operations.

Lee's unit participated in that offensive action. On May 9, his position was overrun. Lee was making his way out to a perimeter position to tend to one of his wounded soldiers when he was cut down by machine gun fire and killed. Because he had been deep in enemy territory in Cambodia, his body did not arrive in Salt Lake City until Wednesday, May 20.

During the five days between Thursday, May 14th and Monday, May 18th, I had three dreams about Lee on three successive nights. The first night I saw Lee dressed in white, sitting on a chair, smiling and looking off into a darkened area. I awoke disturbed and couldn't figure out what it meant. The next night I saw everything I had seen the night before, but as I looked into the darkened area, a small light grew bigger and brighter as it approached Lee. He was still sitting on the chair only this time he reached out his arms as if to embrace someone. I awoke

Some, admiring what motives to mirth infants meet with in their silent and solitary smiles, have resolved...that then they converse with angels!

—*Thomas Fuller,*
A Pisgah-Sight of Palestine

again and still couldn't figure out what it meant or why I should be having these dreams. On the third night I saw everything as I had the two previous nights only this time within the light that was coming out of the darkened area was a little girl with green-blue eyes and beautiful, radiant, blonde hair. She had curls all around her face and was absolutely the most stunning child I had ever seen. She ran into Lee's outstretched arms. He picked her up, placed her on his knee and began telling her about me, my wife and our home. Then with a sudden burst of excitement I realized he was talking to my little girl. He laughed and joked with her and she giggled and accepted his teasing. I awoke with tears streaming down my cheeks and realized I had seen the spirit of our unborn baby and Lee had given her final instructions before she was born.

Cherilee's birth announcement appeared in the *Deseret News* on May 19, 1970, two days before Lee's obituary.

One of my most cherished possessions is a picture of Cherilee with blonde, curly, bouncy hair and shining, laughing, green-blue eyes; the same little girl I saw with my friend Lee.

—*Roy Caldwell*

You were preserved to come to the earth in this time for a special purpose. Not just a few of you, but all of you. There are things for each of you to do that no one else can co as well as you. If you will let Him, I testify that our Father in Heaven will walk with you through the journey of life and inspire you to know your special purpose here.

—*H. Burke Peterson, "Your Life Has a Purpose,"* New Era, *May 1979, pp. 4-5.*

"I Don't Want to Come Before My Time"

My husband has a very tender heart for those in need—similar to the little boy who brings home a stray puppy dog. But my husband doesn't bring home puppies; he brings home people. Through his work he has met several people who have needed a home, either temporarily or for an extended period of time.

About eleven years ago, with my permission, he brought home Ellen, a fifteen-year-old girl who had experienced abuse. Ellen was very shy at first and wore her bangs so long that you could not see her eyes. She seemed to be emotionally hiding from us, and in reality she was hiding from life in general.

Within the first week, Ellen began to gain trust in us. Soon she approached us and very timidly confessed that she was afraid she was pregnant. Her young boyfriend was a disarrayed and confused young man. We

To A Child

*Do you know who you are—little
    child of mine—
So precious and dear to me?
Do you know you're a part of a
    great design
That is vast as eternity?
Can you think for a moment how
    much depends
On your holding the "Iron Rod"?
Your life is forever—worlds with-
    out end—
Do you know you're a child of
    God?
Do you know where you've been,
    little child of mine?
It is hard to recall, I know;
Do you ever remember that Home
    divine
With the Father who loves you
    so?*

—Ora Pate Stewart

were very concerned about her.

As the three of us knelt in prayer and beseeched the Lord for guidance, my husband felt impressed that she needed a blessing by the laying on of hands.

During this blessing, as my husband spoke the words, a scene or vision appeared in my mind. I saw Ellen sitting on the green grass in front of a beautiful church or chapel with her husband. They were both dressed in wedding attire; Helen in a beautiful white dress, and the young man in a brown suit, similar to the color of his hair. I distinctly saw his form and features. Their faces were radiant with their joy and love. This vision faded and I saw a new one. I saw Ellen with a beautiful baby. She was holding this baby up in the air with her arms outstretched as if thanking God in heaven for this wonderful gift. It was apparent that this child had come to her after her marriage to the young man in the vision.

Time soon proved that she was not pregnant. She began to blossom in her new growth and opportunities and her shyness was replaced with an exuberant teen-age energy. One day she began to prepare for a date with a young man in our neighborhood. When the doorbell rang, she answered and invited Ken to wait on the couch while she grabbed her purse. As I greeted Ken and began to talk with him, suddenly I had a strange realization. This was the young man I had seen with Ellen in the vision.

As Ken and Ellen began to date, even though they were very young, they soon fell in love. Ellen told me about a feeling they had while on a hike of "deja vu" in which they both suddenly had strong impressions that they had known each other before in a previous time, even before earth life.

One evening as I slept, whether in a dream or vision, I know not, a young woman came to my bedside. Her message to me was clear, "Tell Mom and Dad to be careful. I don't want to come before my time." I recognized this young woman to be Ellen's unborn child.

The following day I approached Ellen and asked her if she was being careful in her physical relationship with Ken. Were they honoring the values that my husband and I and our church had taught her? She acknowledged that they had slipped somewhat but promised me that they would honor these values from now on. They were true to this commitment and developed a great love and respect for one another which was mature beyond their years.

Little Baby

Little baby yet unborn
In my womb so safe and warm
Living with me who will you be?
Living with me I wish I could see

My little baby yet unborn
In my womb so safe and warm.

—*Dana and Damien Scallon,*
© *August Music,*
Heart Beat Records
Birmingham, AL
Used with Permission

In the years that followed, Ellen moved back home. Ken left on an extended trip and they were planning their engagement when he returned. One afternoon the door-bell rang. It was Ellen. She looked very lost and forsaken. I hardly recognized her because her contagious enthusiasm was missing.

"I am so lonely without Ken," she said. "I am not sure I can wait until he gets home. I've met another man who has proposed marriage and even though I've had dreams warning me not to do it, I'm going to marry him."

I was shocked. I reminded Ellen of the previous experiences I had received concerning her and Ken. "Please, wait, at least until Ken gets home. It's just a matter of a few months until you will be with him again."

"I can't," she said. "I feel like I'm in a downward spiral and I just can't get out of it."

She asked my husband for another blessing. As he blessed her, he told her that negative forces were trying to block her eventual reunion with Ken. She needed to wait until Ken returned home before she made a decision who to marry. During this blessing I saw a young woman standing in the middle of our living room. She was wringing her hands as if she were extremely worried.

MOTHER

Joyful to perpetuate the plan,
To procreate,
I rejoice in choice to be a Mother.

—LeAnne Townsend
© Copyright 1987

She said, "Tell Mom not to marry this man. It's wrong."

After the blessing, Ellen left so rapidly I didn't have time to tell her about my experience. I phoned her the following day, which was Mother's Day. She invited me to her home where we could talk privately. After I told her about my experience with the young woman wringing her hands, she broke down and cried.

"You're right," she said. "I'll wait for Ken to return before I make any decisions."

The young man to whom she was considering marriage soon stepped out of her life, and within a few months, Ken was home. Their marriage plans progressed rapidly. In the meanwhile, my husband's work had taken us 2,000 miles away. What a joy for us to hear about their wedding day and to share in their happiness. A year later, a beautiful baby girl was born to them.

A recent reunion with them after many years of being apart confirmed our hopes. My husband and I were thrilled as we watched them as a small family with two little girls, their unity so apparent. Truly the Lord had plans for these two people to be together with their children as a family forever and eternal.

—Elaine S.

We frequently say, "How familiar that person's face is to me." In this way kindred spirits are brought together. We are drawn together by this knowledge and this acquaintanceship which, I have no doubt, was formed anterior to our birth in this state of existence.

—George Q. Cannon, in Deseret Weekly, (Salt Lake City, April 7, 1889), 38: pp. 676-677.

[1]*Opening the Windows of Heaven* by Carol Jeanne Ehlers and Vicki Jo Robinson, (Salt Lake City, Utah: Hawkes Publishing, Inc., 1987), p. 43.

[2]IBID, p. 40.

[3]IBID, pp. 37-38.

[4]Richard G. Ellsworth, "Growing Toward the Good," *The New Era*, (May 1986), pp. 8-10, (Salt Lake City, Utah), used with permission.

[5]*Opening the Windows of Heaven* by Carol Jeanne Ehlers and Vicki Jo Robinson, (Salt Lake City, Utah: Hawkes Publishing, Inc., 1987), pp. 43-44.

[6]Cheryl Cayer, as told to Judy M. Sweeney, Edmonton, Alberta, Canada, *Ensign*, (July 1992), p.56, (Salt Lake City, Utah), used with permission.

[7]*Opening the Windows of Heaven* by Carol Jeanne Ehlers and Vicki Jo Robinson, (Salt Lake City, Utah: Hawkes Publishing, Inc., 1987), p. 38.

[8]*Daughters of God* by Carol Jeanne Ehlers, Vicki Jo Robinson and Elisa M. Newbold (Salt Lake City, Utah: Hawkes Publishing, Inc., 1981), pp. 97-98.

[9]*Opening the Windows of Heaven* by Carol Jeanne Ehlers and Vicki Jo Robinson, (Salt Lake City, Utah: Hawkes Publishing, Inc., 1987), pp. 41-42.

My Feelings as a Reader Concerning These Experiences

If, after reading these accounts, you are aware of a similar experience that you think would be an appropriate addition to the growing body of evidence that the human soul lives beyond this mortal life, both before birth and after death, we invite you to tell us about the account. Please send either type written pages or a cassette tape recording for our review for possible use in future editions.

Please include appropriate addresses and phone numbers in the event we wish to obtain permission to publish your experience.

Send possible contributions for future editions to:

Publisher

Cedar Fort, Inc.

925 North Main Street

Springville, UT 84663